Publisher's Note

The book descriptions we ask booksellers to display prominently warn that this is an historic book with numerous typos, missing text or index and is not illustrated.

We scanned this book using character recognition software that includes an automated spell check. Our software is 99 percent accurate if the book is in good condition. However, we do understand that even less than one percent can be a very annoying number of typos! And sometimes all or part of a page is missing from our copy of a book. Or the paper may be so discolored from age that you can no longer read the type. Please accept our sincere apologies.

After we re-typeset and design a book, the page numbers change so the old index and table of contents no longer work. Therefore, we usually remove them.

Our books sell so few copies that you would have to pay hundreds of dollars to cover the cost of proof reading and fixing the typos, missing text and index. Therefore, whenever possible, we let our customers download a free copy of the original typo-free scanned book. Simply enter the barcode number from the back cover of the paperback in the Free Book form at www.general-books. net. You may also qualify for a free trial membership in our book club to download up to four books for free. Simply enter the barcode number from the back cover onto the membership form on the same page. The book club entitles you to select from more than a million books at no additional charge. Simply enter the title or subject onto the search form to find the books.

If you have any questions, could you please be so kind as to consult our Frequently Asked Questions page at www. general-books.net/faqs.cfm? You are also welcome to contact us there.

General Books LLC™, Memphis, USA, 2012. ISBN: 9781151577665.

❄❄ ❄❄ ❄❄ ❄❄ ❄❄ ❄❄ ❄❄ ❄❄

FORTUNE-TELLING is not so difficult as some people imagine, for is it not true that
"Feathers show how the wind blows,
And straws tell how the current flows"?

And is it not also true that, in some shape, we have all our *straws* and *feathers,* which give to the observing and experienced such insight into our character, as enables them to foretell, with tolerable certainty, what will befall us in after-days? For instance, I never see a man spending his money and time in a public house, but I know that man is sowing dragon's teeth, and will have a terrible harvest; nor do I ever see a woman neglecting her own household duties to gossip with her neighbours, but I know her children are not likely to call her blessed. I never see a young lad with a cigar or short pipe in his mouth, who has turned his back on the church or the Sunday-school, and can talk about his father as the " old governor," and his mother as the "old woman," trying to make himself look big by scoffing at things serious, but I know that young man is mixing a bitter cup for somebody, but one more bitter still for himself. Nor do I ever see a young woman decked in showy finery, trying to attract everybody's notice,—preferring Sunday walks to Sunday Bchools, places of amusement to places of worship, and foolish companions to fireside duties,—but I am certain that sorrow is close at her heels. I know not how many books have been written on fortune-telling, but I know of one book that tells fortunes with amazing certainty; and in one passage it declares, that What We sow We Must Also Reap. One illustration of this unerring truth, we give in the following narrative.

Some of my readers will remember that, in my younger years, I resided in a village just outside the town of Kochdale, called Cut-Gate. In this village there was one public house and two grocer's shops. One of these shops was kept by an elderly widow, of consider-able energy and spirit; and, to help her in the business and household affairs, she obtained the assistance of a relative, a young female about nineteen or twenty years of age.

The appearance of this young woman in our rural hamlet, caused a little stir amongst its inhabitants; for in most villages, everybody knows everybody, looks after everybody, and minds everybody's business, sometimes better than their own. Had she gone to reside in some large town, she might have lived and died without her next-door neighbour knowing her name. But not so in our group of country cottages. We all soon knew that her aunt called her Nanny, and the young women soon knew that she held her head a little above any of them, besides outstripping them in her style of dress; for she was often seen in light, showy gowns, curls or ringlets, and a large scalloped shell comb to fasten up her back hair. One or two girls, the most foolish in the village, bought large combs, and tried to curl their hair like Nanny, but none of them could compete with her. This caused not a little envy and mortification.

But it was not our females only that were influenced by the new arrival; for some of the young men began to pull up their shirt-collars, stretch down their coattails, and pay more than usual attention to the brushing of their hats and shoes, with a distant hope that they might not be entirely overlooked. After some time, one of these young men was seen arm-in-arm with Nanny, taking a Sunday walk; and from that time it was generally understood that Kobert and Nanny were engaged.

One fine Sunday afternoon, almost all the inhabitants of our village turned out to see what, perhaps, had never been seen amongst us before. Two horses, saddled and bridled, stood at the grocer's door—one with a lady's side-saddle on. While the children were gathered round the horses, and the villagers stood at their doors looking for the riders, out came Robert and Nanny, both finer than we had ever seen them before. He had on a white waistcoat, and she a long, light dress, and more curls than ever. He assisted her to mount, and both set off at a canter, quite astonishing every one of us; for all were looking on with open eyes and mouth. When they had got out of sight, one old woman exclaimed,—

"Well, that caps all! If Robert weds yon lass, drapers will have to give him long credit."

"Yes," replied another, "he will not need to go to old Thaniel to have his fortin toud. I con tell him mysel."

"Has she ony brass, I wonder?" observed the first speaker.

"Brass! Not her, indeed. I asked her aunt, and she said she was as poor as me; and I am poor enough, everybody knows," replied the other. "Besides, what can *he* have *1* He is only a working man. Twice nought is nought, and nought will not keep folks on. horseback."

It was about this period that the circumstance took place which gives the title to this narrative. The cottage in which I resided was two doors from the grocer's shop. One room next to the shop was used as a warehouse, and behind this room was a small place, called the parlour. One afternoon, when I was about seven years of age, I was helping in the warehouse, and was terribly frightened by a loud scream in the little parlour. I ran to see the cause, and there stood Nanny, the very picture of despair, looking at a large lock of her hair that lay, along with the curling tongs, on the floor. Her aunt, having also heard the scream, came running to see what was the matter. Seeing the lock of hair on the floor, she began to scold her niece, declaring that, if she had been a minute, she had been two hours before the glass curling; and, if she lived, she would have something more to scream about than the loss of a few hairs from her head. Nanny, full of indignation, turned round to the glass, and began combing out her hair for a fresh start, minding, however, not to have the curling-tongs too hot the next time, lest she

might burn off another precious curl.

Soon after this event, the village was all astir to gaze at a rather merry wedding party, going and returning from the church, and again the wise people were making their predictions. One old man wondered how long it was since either bride or bridegroom had been inside a church before; observing that he wished them much happiness, but something more than a wish was required to make people happy.

This merry wedding party was that of Eobert and Nanny. I have no objection to people being merry j I like to see proper mirth and joy; but I do think, if there be one day in our lives that is an important day, H is that on which we link our destiny with one who will be to us a blessing or a curse. A fiddling wedding is very often a foolish wedding.

For several months after the marriage, the young couple seemed all right, but it was remarked that Eobert did not attend so well to his work as formerly. The reason of this was, he intended to change to some other business or trade, for his new wife did not think a blacksmith was sufficiently respectable; and at her persuasion he left the forge, and commenced business as a wholesale dealer in malt.

Eespectable, indeed! Is not all useful labour respectable J Is there not a real dignity in such labour I Many a man who, through pride, has left honourable employment for questionable speculation, after having his high notions rolled in the mud, has been glad to creep back to his true position. "Respectable is, as respectable does," is a maxim which applies to every grade of society.

Soon after entering into the malt trade, it was evident to all that knew Robert that a great change was coming over him. From being sprightly and cheerful, he became silent and thoughtful. To get custom, he spent much time in public houses, and this soon began to tell on his appearance. He began to prefer the public house to his own. He was deficient in what all dealers in malt especially require—self-control; and very soon malt controlled him, as it has controlled millions. Oh, that malt! that

malt! If one could collect the myriads of wretched children, whose pale faces are smitten by early sorrow, or stamped with the impress of early crime, and ask them why they are in rags, tatters, and tears, the answer would be "Malt!" If one could stand on the top of St. Paul's, and shout with a voice that could be heard in every miserable home in England, and ask, "Why are you miserable?" the answer from thousands of breaking hearts would be "Malt!" Or if the same voice, turning to the hundreds of prisons, with their almost countless ruined inmates, should ask why these pests of mankind are chained, behind locks, bolts, and bars, the response would be " Malt!" Or if we could stand on the brink of perdition, and ask the lost souls what brought them into that place of endless woe, the reply from doomed millions, like the roaring of many thunders, would be "Malt!" No tongue, no pen can ever describe what misery, ruin, sorrow, and crime MALT has produced.

Eobert, finding he was sinking in health and circumstances, wished to give up his destructive business; but no! his proud wife would not hear a word of it. For, though she knew that his credit was bad, still she kept up her style of dress and showy appearance; and he, like many a poor, struggling husband, had a millstone hung round his neck, by a foolish, showy, proud wife; as many a hard-working, honest father has been made to carry continual sorrow, through the extravagance and vanity of proud, showy daughters.

I have often been pained, both in our churches and chapels, by seeing the dignity, pomp, style, and evident self-admiration with which many of these gaily dressed females enter the house dedicated to humble devotion and prayer, as if God Almighty were indebted to them for coming, and to hear them afterwards descanting on the dresses, and especially the bonnets, of those that were present.

"Did you see Mrs. and Miss Edwards at the church yesterday?" asks one.

"Yes; what style! How did you like their bonnets?" asks another.

"Not very well; I don't think peach trimmings suit her complexion; mauve, or magenta would do much better."

"Did you see Mrs. Phillips? She likes plenty of colour in her trimmings. Is her husband doing much business?"

"I don't know, but I think he should be, for she costs no little to keep up her pomp, for

They have the longest bills
Who wear the most frills."

"What was the text on Sunday morning? for I have quite forgot," asks the first speaker.

"Well, you are as bad as me, for I don't remember the text, or much of the sermon, only it was something about the Jews."

This is only a small sample of what may be heard every week, from a class of persons who seem to consider the church as only a place for showing fashions; and it is quite time that ministers of the Gospel speak out on the question, for some of our sanctuaries are becoming places of gaiety, almost as much as the ball-room.

While I do not believe in a religious dress—for I don't think religion consists in the shape of either coat, hat, or bonnet—yet I am persuaded that, as a rule, the dress is an indication of the mind.

If one quarter of the time was spent in adorning the heart, and in thoughtful preparation for the worship of the sanctuary, that is spent before the glass, in decking and adorning the frail, dying body, heaven would gain many precious souls that will never enter there; for, I firmly believe that many of our females think more about the shape of their bonnet, than the salvation of their soul.

Isaiah spake of such in his day. Walking with wanton eyes; mincing as they go; with chains, bracelets, and mufflers; head-bands, tablets, and ear-rings ; mantles, wimples, and crisping pins. These had all their doom predicted. It came, and come it ever will, for "the Lord hateth a proud look." How immeasurably must such a tawdry thing be below the beauty mentioned by Paul—adorned in modest apparel; not with broidered hair, or gold, or pearls, or costly array, but with modesty and good works. Isaiah's mincers have ruined thousands; Paul's beauties never one. They are no expensive shams, but ornaments and blessings to every husband, every father, and every home. They are infinitely to be preferred, as wives, to mantles, wimples, and crisping pins, and will be preferred by every sensible man. Well had it been for Robert had he chosen such a wife.

Robert's malt business was a failure. His circumstances became desperate, and, to escape from the consequence, he fled to America, leaving his wife to do as she could. No doubt he did wrong here, but people in desperate circumstances cannot always reason. After he left, the shop was broken up, her husband's father took the two children, and for many months Nanny lived amongst her few friends. But she was in good health, and, had she bent her mind to her circumstances, as noble souls ever will, she might have found some honourable way of earning her bread. This she was too proud to do, however. Her friends, seeing this, one by one cast her off, and she was again left to fight her own battle.

She now removed to Bolton, and for some time was u lost sight of. But it appears that her love of finery was still her ruling passion; for, on reading the papers, many of us were startled by seeing an account of her imprisonment for stealing a shawl and a pair of boots. The evidence against her was so conclusive, that she was sent to Liverpool, there to await her trial at the assizes.

Poor Nanny, how sad was I when I heard of thy disgrace, thy dreadful fall, and thy impending fate. I could have wept, and gone to speak a word of comfort to thee; for well I remembered how, in my boyish days, thou patted my young cheek, and gave me many a penny to take thy sealed letters to thy now self-banished husband. With my child's heart I loved thee, and thought thee a fine lady; and when, in my innocence, I picked up the hot tongs that burned off thy lost curl, I felt a wish to put back thy lock of hair, if I could have done so. As my young heart wished for thee then, so do I wish for thee now, that thou hadst gone to some dear place of worship, some house of prayer, and, in meekness of spirit, bowed before thy God, and sought peace with Him through Jesus Christ. He would have saved thee, and guarded thee, and, instead of being immured in thy silent, gloomy prison cell, thou wouldst have been a happy child of God on earth, or a blessed saint in heaven.

The day of trial came: the heralds, lawyers, and jury came: and, with whatever indifference mere spectators may regard an assize day, to those whose fate hangs on that day, and whose hearts almost die within them when the trumpet sounds to tell the judge is coming, it is a very different thing. I have witnessed many such scenes, but never without remembering that another and a last trump will sound, and then the Judge will come to judge us all.

I have often thought of poor Nanny's condition on the day of her trial. It is pitiable enough to be imprisoned for crime, but it is sad indeed to be without one loving heart, or one single friend in the wide, wide world. To love, and to be loved, is true life. God is love, and the source of love; and the more we love, and especially the more we love Him, the more we are like Him. The devil cannot love, and those who are most like the devil love the least.

When Nanny was brought from the cell to the dock, she held down her head in shame and sorrow. All eyes were fixed upon her, and when the counsel for the crown laid before the judge and jury the crushing evidence of her crime, there was no reply; she had no one to defend her, and the verdict against her was "Guilty!"

The judge lifted his head from a paper he was reading, and, in a voice of tenderness, said, "My young woman, have you any one in the court who can say anything in your favour ?" No answer.

Again he asked, "Have you no one present to speak one word for you ?" Nanny shook her head, but gave no answer.

A third time he asked, looking round

the court, if there was no person fiat knew her, that could say anything in her behalf? Still no answer!

He paused for a moment, and then, in slow, distinct words, said, "My young woman, the sentence against you is, that you be transported beyond the sea for seven years."

One wild, piercing shriek, which sent a thrill of pain through the entire court, and Nanny fell senseless in the arms of the jailor.

Soon after she returned to consciousness, one of the prison officials, with a large pair of scissors in his hand, came to cut her hair to the length allowed by prison rules. Crash! crash! went the shears through her yet long, beautiful tresses, and the poor creature was made to look like a felon indeed; but she did not resent it—she did not complain, or shed one tear, while her hair was being cut away. Deep sorrow had entered her soul—she was humbled to the dust—she was meek as a little child. Did she now remember her aunt's prediction?

A few weeks after, the transport ship came, and the transport ship went. Many on board that ship had, like Nanny, darkened their future prospects by early follies and early crimes; and, like her, were receiving the wages of sin, having inflicted on themselves and others unspeakable trouble. Oh, how many breaking hearts have followed the wake of the transport ship! How many sobbing or wailing partings, never to meet again? Early and continued piety would prevent these dreadful scenes. If none but the true Christian—the really religious—were imprisoned, transported, or hanged, every transport ship would rot, every prison would tumble into ruins, and the drop and beam of every gallows moulder to dust, before they would have one single soul for a victim.

We know little of poor, exiled Nanny after she left her native land; only that she became very meek, obedient, and kind to every one, and that she made many friends on the passage out, and when she reached her destination. We also heard that she never smiled, but often read her Bible; that her health failed her, and she gradually sunk into a com-

paratively early tomb. Her body now sleeps in a distant settlement and in a foreign grave, but we trust that her bruised soul, renewed by Divine grace, is gone to where graves and penal settlements are unknown.

Poor Nanny! thou art not the only one that a foolish love of extravagant finery has dragged down to infamy and irretrievable ruin; thousands, like thee, have had to wail, in after-life, over character, friends, virtue, peace, and hope all gone—gone, never to return, in this world. And yet, this fearful whirlpool is still sucking down its thousands, who are bent on indulging in this destructive infatuation. Would that thy example might prevent some poor, erring creature from following in thy fatal wake; then the object of this narrative will be answered.

Who communicated to Eobert the intelligence of his wife's banishment we knew not, but we know he returned from America some time after she was gone. Ho was greatly changed, and changed for the worse—malt was still doing its dreadful work. He was never heard to mention his wife, or to make the slightest allusion to her; not even when madly raving under *delirium tremens,* as he often was. We also know that in one of these truly fearful conditions, with reeling reason and burning brain, he wandered wildly over a neighbouring moor, where he had often played in his happy, innocent childhood, and, in that frightful state of mind and body, he leaped into the deep, cold waters of Lumb, near the valley of Cheesden.

I have this day, October 27th, 1865, stood on the bank from which, in his moment of madness, he plunged into the dark, deep waters, and this day talked with his near neighbour, Henry Howarth, who often tried to calm him in those hours of madness, and who, after the inquest, brought his dead body to the house from which he helped to carry it to its last resting-place, about thirty feet from the centre of the east window, in the grave of his grandmother, in Spotland church-yard.

Poor Robert! poor Nanny! Silks and

satins, mantles, wimples, crisping-pins, and malt have done their gloomy work for you, as they have done for thousands: and never, while memory lasts, shall I forget the lesson taught me by her who is the principal subject of this narrative. The prophecy of her aunt has been bitterly fulfilled—that prophecy uttered on the day Nanny screamed over her lock of hair—her burned Lost Curl.

AS you enter the town of Oldham, from the Mumps Railway Station, near the baths in Union Street, there is a small cottage numbered 60. For many years the windows of this cottage had been filled with cigars, tobacco, fruit, sweetmeats, sporting papers, and infidel publications; but on the Sabbath the window was decked out with all possible attention, to allure and corrupt the young or old people in the neighbourhood.

Having a Sabbath engagement in Oldham, I informed the gentleman in whose house I was staying on the Saturday evening, that I should probably let myself out early in the morning to take a quiet walk through the streets, to have a little conversation with the stragglers and groups of street loungers, and try if I could induce some of them to get washed and attend a place of worship.

Passing down Union Street about seven the following morning, I came to this open toffy-shop. A middleaged woman was on her knees washing the door-step. Wishing to speak to her, I stooped down and said,—

"My good woman, have you any money in the Savings' Bank?"

The woman rose from her knees, with the floor-cloth in her hand, and, looking me in the face, said,—

"What ever made you ax me that, felley *V*

"Well, Mrs.," I replied, "I have been asking that question of many Sunday shopkeepers for the last twenty years, and I have never found one that had saved anything; they are all a poor, poverty-stricken lot, and I am anxious to know if you are like the rest I have seen."

"Us aught saved? Nay, not us. I wish we had," she again replied.

Just then a tall, thia man came across

the street, and, looking me rather fierce-ly in the face, said,—

"What are you saying to my wife?"

"Well, sir, if this be your wife, I have been asking her if you have any money in the bank?" I replied.

"Ah! you are one of the black coats, are you? Where is your white choker?" he asked.

"I do not happen to have one on at present, but I have a black coat of good Yorkshire oloth. Just rub your hand down the sleeve and feel how smooth it is."

This playful expression on my part rather changed his temper, but again ad-dressing me with an important air, he. observed,—

"You have caught a tartar this morn-ing, and one that has had many a twist with such chaps as you, for if there is aught I delight in, it is to choke a par-son. I wish I could choke them every one, so that they could never speak again."

"What sort of a tartar are you?" I asked.

"My name is Emmott, a well-known secularist of thirty years' standing."

"Then I am not surprised at your keeping a Sunday Bhop, and wanting to strangle parsons," I replied.

"Say what you will, I shall keep this little shop ,open when I like, and I have a good reason for keeping it open on the Sunday, and I can clinch it with an ar-gument you cannot touch."

"Well, what is your clincher?"

"Why, that I can make about two shillings out of the goods in that win-dow to-day, and two shillings are two shillings. If I was to go to the Guardians for two shillings I might have to stand waiting two hours, and be snubbed in the bargain."

"Well, sir, I admire your spirit as re-gards going to the Guardians, for I have no patience with persons going for parish relief that can help it. Some are forced to go, but many go that might do without it, if they would only make an effort. But I think your argument a very lame one, for Sunday shopkeepers are far more likely to find their way to the poor-house in the long run than persons

that honour the Sabbath."

"Why, how do you make that out?"

"Well, sir, here you have your fruit, toffy, and penny cigars, to say nothing about your infidel books, tempting Sun-day-school scholars, and inducing them to do what their parents and teachers warn them against doing. You sell these cigars and tobacco to mere boys, help-ing them to form degrading habits, and thereby injuring your neighbours' chil-dren. The consequence will be, that re-spectable people will not trade with you any day, for, depend upon it, society is a social compact. Despise and snub so-ciety, and it will despise and snub you; respect and smile at it and it will respect and smile at you. To make this more clear, did you ever see a six-foot look-ing glass %"

"Yes, many a one."

"Well, the next time you see one, stand before it, clench your fist, and, with a look of defiance, say, 'Who cares for *jouV* and you will see one with clenched fist and defiant look saying, 'Who cares for youT But if you smile and say, 'Good morning, my friend, I wish you prosperity,' you will see one smiling in return, and wishing you pros-perity. Now, sir, this is society, and what you measure to it, you will have measured back. A man must, in this re-spect, reap what he sows."

During this conversation we had en-tered the house. He folded his arms, leaned against an old mangle, and seemed in a deep study, then looking at his wife, said,—

"Do you hear what this man says, lass? I think there is some weight in it, for I have been snubbing and defying society for the last thirty years, and it has nearly snubbed us both into the workhouse. I think I will try smiling,— here goes,"—and Emmott swept toffy, tobacco, cigars, and infidel papers all out of the window, putting them on the top of the mangle, and pulled down his blind,—his wife staring at him with the greatest astonishment all the while.

While Emmott's wife was gazing at him in wonder, I was watching his pro-ceedings with pleasure, and when he had finished, I said,—

"Well done! and depend upon it you will be commercially a gainer. Now, if you keep a correct account of your deal-ings, I shall, all well, be coming this way again, and I dare venture to make up all you lose, if you will give me your gains; and, now, what do you say to go-ing to some place of worship?"

"Nay, nay! Your looking-glass argu-ment has knocked me down, for I be-lieve it, but no churches or chapels for me. Oldham folks will be amazed enough to see the shop shut up, but they will never see me in a church. I see by the bills on the walls that John Ash-worth of Rochdale is going to preach in the chapel at the end of the street. I did think once of going to hear what that chap had to say. I have read his 'Wilkins,' 'Sanderson,' and 'Niff and his Dogs,' and long for a chance of just meeting that meddling fool."

"Well, sir, if you will get ready, I will call on you about the time, and we will go together."

"No, no! Chapels and churches are nought in my line—I wish they were all in ruins; besides, my Sunday jump is in the popshop, and I shall not go in these rags."

When I returned to the house at which I was staying, and, during break-fast, recounted to the gentleman and his wife the adventures of the morning— more especially my conversation with Emmott—they were greatly surprised and pleased. I expressed a wish that he might be visited by a few judicious friends, to encourage him giving up his Sunday trading, and I thought it possi-ble that he might yet be induced to at-tend some place of worship. This was done by Messrs. Mortimer, Hibbert, and others, for they all became interested in Emmott's case.

How mysterious are the ways of Him whose path ways are in the deep! with infinite love and pity He looks on our fallen humanity, and, though there is no other name by which we can be saved but the name of,Christ Jesus, yet many and various influences are at work in-tended to bring wicked men to seek sal-vation in that name, and to trust in the goodness of God. Bruce, the traveller, when dying in despair on the arid sands of the Abyssinian desert, was led to trust in God's providence from seeing a small green plant blooming amidst the sands. Linnaeus, the naturalist, fell on his knees before the common English gorse, and thanked God he had been spared to see this additional evidence of His wisdom. I know a poor woman who, almost broken-hearted with sorrow, sat weeping beside a well; a little girl was plucking daisies and blue-bells, and singing "Come to Jesus;" the woman heard the child's song, knelt down and sought comfort from that Jesus of whom the child was singing, and from that day became a happy Christian.

The singing of a lark was amongst the influences that melted down the haughty spirit of Emmott. Soon after my visit he was walking through Oldham park; a lark was just rising from the ground; he watched it as it ro'se higher and higher, warbling its sweet notes as it ascended, till it became a mere speck in the clear blue sky. "Yes," said Emmott to himself, "yon little bird is filled with song and joy, while I am miserable and wretched. This winged creature, a mere thing of instinct, warbles and basks in the sunbeam, answering the purposes of its existence, and is happy . but I, a rational creature, am gloomy and sad of heart. How is this? If there be a God He must have as much regard for my happiness as for the happiness of that bird *1* That bird sings its song without snubbing or insulting its fellows, or denying its Maker. It needs not to look into the six-foot glass to teach it that like must produce like."

These reflections brought tears, and Emmott caught himself offering up a prayer, that he too might answer the purpose of his existence, and become a happy man; and, strange as it may seem, that prayer was the verse of a hymn taught him by his mother—a mother that had offered many prayers for her wayward son, but for thirty years he had never even thought of it—but now that mother's verse—

"Come, holy Spirit, from above,
Impart Thy gift of grace and love;

Visit me with celestial fire,
And with Thyself my soul inspire," became the involuntary language of a burdened soul.

The Sabbath following found Emmott in the house of prayer. Again and again he sought the sanctuary, and in tears of penitence besought Him whom he had denied and insulted to have mercy upon him, and pardon the most guilty of all guilty sinners. He was in this state of mind when he sent me the following letter:

"60, Union Street, Oldham, Oct. 24, 1864. "Kind Friend,

"I little thought when you came to my door the other Sunday morning, that I should have so soon to plead for God's mercy—me that had so often denied His existence—but such is the fact. O Mr. Ashworth that I could but undo the injury that my principles and conduct have done, I might have some hope of yet being happy. Had it not been that the Lord directed you to my house, I should have been lost. Will you pray for me, and, if you can, soon come to see me? Yours very sincerely,

"RICHD-EMMOTT."

On my calling to see Emmott, I was much surprised to find him so greatly changed. He requested me to remain with him as long as I possibly could, and take down in writing what he wanted to say. He then gave me the following sketch of his wayward life, which I give in his own words:—

"My earliest recollections are connected with Skipton-in-Craven. Then I went to the Sunday school, but left when ten years of age. When about twenty, I lived in Bradford, and it was then I became an infidel, from reading Carlisle's "Destructive." I joined the Chartists, bought a gun and bayonet, but had to flee from the neighbourhood to escape imprisonment. I enlisted for a soldier, and had to stand guard over the jail containing three of our leaders—Frost, Williams, and Jones. This I did not like, and deserted. I travelled six hundred miles in women's clothes, but was caught, and I am now marked with the letter D. I came to live in Manchester, and joined a company of low-lived

infidels, and soon became so degraded, that my wife left me and came to Oldham. I followed her, and again found several of the same class, but calling themselves secularists. About this time I was perfectly savage against everyone professing religion, and took every opportunity of insulting them. I would not touch, or allow my child to touch the Bible, though I have flogged him because he would not tell a lie. I drove the Biblesellers out of the Market-place by turning all they said into ridicule, and laughed and mocked at all the open-air preachers I could find. Many of them, especially young, inexperienced men, I have driven away, by asking obscene questions they could not or durst not answer.

"I once pushed a donkey into a prayer-meeting, telling the astonished company that I had brought them a sinner to be converted, that had as much a soul as any of them.

"I was once sick, and, at my sister's request, a minister came to see me. He was taking out his Bible to read, but I told him to put away the cursed book, and find me two flannel shirts, which would do me more good than all the Bibles or prayers in the world. He replied that God could send blessings for the body as well as the soul; but I told him he was a liar, for God did not deal in flannel, if there was a God.

"I never heard a church bell but I wished the ground would open and swallow up all the churches and chapels with the parsons, and I gloated in keeping open shop and selling sporting and infidel publications on the Sunday. Such has been my life for thirty years.

"I have been in many towns, and amongst all classes of infidels, especially the secularists. Some of these pretend to be rather more respectable than the old stock of infidels, but they are all a miserable, wretched lot—a withering blight follows aught they take in hand. They are an organization without a head, a body without a substance, denying the existence of a God, and are without faith in man. Rejecting the moral law, they laugh at all moral responsibility, and are only kept in order by the laws of the country. Most secularists are better than their creed, for, did they practise what they pretend to believe, society would become impossible; and I believe with Gordon, one of their late lecturers, 'That a secularist, to gain his own point, can commit the most horrid crimes, even murder, and be consistent with his principles.' It is a mercy that mankind holds their principles in abhorrence, and that such a race of beings are almost extinct.

"When my eyes were opened, and I saw how great a sinner I was, I felt greatly troubled about the injury I had done to others by the sale of infidel publications those passports to ruin, and resolved that not one more should pass through my hands or remain in my house. I gathered them all together, with the books belonging to myself, costing in all about four pounds; I piled them on the fire, and, as I saw them consuming in the flames, I felt as if I was burning the devil, and watched their destruction with the greatest pleasure. Now, thought I, you are done for.

"Since this change came over my mind, my home is already like a paradise to what it was. Now, I have a quiet, peaceable home; before it was like a bedlam, especially on the Sunday. Then it was filled with all sorts of rabble, talking all sorts of wicked, filthy talk, from morning to night. Never was there such a change in a house, and I hope God will have mercy upon me and pardon my many transgressions, and then it will be a change indeed,—it will be bliss here and hereafter, and an immortality of bliss is bliss."

Emmott finished this short sketch of his life by requesting me to provide him with a Bible, that he might read it day and night. He also requested that I would couple our names with a date, so that he might be often reminded of the time and circumstances that had brought us together. I cheerfully complied with his request, and one true sign of a real change is, the book he once mortally hated he now loves. But is there not another sign of an amazing change? No sooner does Emmott emerge from the gloomy cavern of infidelity and catch a ray of heavenly light, but he began to talk about an immortality of bliss!

The change that Emmott was so troubled and anxious about came at last. He had been very attentive at the means of grace on the Sabbath, and requested he might be allowed to attend a weeknight meeting for Christian experience. From one of these meetings he returned in the deepest distress, and for four days sought mercy in prayers and tears. "O Lord, wilt Thou not pardon me *1* If Thou wilt not, I cannot be surprised, for I have laughed Thee to scorn, and thousands of times insulted the very name of Thy dear Son that died for me. I have indeed been the chief of sinners, but wilt Thou not save me? O, do Lord, do; for Christ's sake, that died for sinners, do save me!"

That heart-broken prayer was heard, and again the power of Christ's blood was made manifest in being able to save the chief of sinners, for Emmott became a child of God, a sinner saved by grace.

In a letter I received immediately after, in which he gives this prayer and his deliverance, he says:— "For a moment I felt as if I had left the earth, and that my spirit was soaring aloft into heaven. I felt my faith to be as strong as Samson. My wife says I am as happy as a king, but no king is half so happy. This is the brightest day of my life, and I now truly. begin to live, for I am a child of God, bought with the blood of the Lamb of God, that taketh away the sin of the world. I hope I shall walk humbly before Him, and daily ask His blessing and grace to guide me, and help me to live at peace with all mankind."

Emmott's conversion produced great astonishment amongst all those who knew him in Oldham. That the sneering, mocking, scorning, scoffing, Sunday shopkeeping, infidel bookselling, thirty-year secularist should become a Christian, astonished all, and greatly pleased many, but it was like a bombshell thrown among his old companions in infidelity. Many of these called to see if what they had heard was true, and found it true indeed. But when it was reported that Emmott was expected to give a public confession of his conversion at the church he attended, many went who are not often found in a place of worship.

This service, Mr. Mortimer, the minister, opened with singing, prayer, and a short address. Several of the members spoke a few words, but when Emmott rose, with evident nervousness, all eyes were turned towards him, with the most intense interest and in breathless silence. His first words were feeble and tremulous. He spoke of the amazing goodness of God in preserving his life during the many years of his wicked career, and mourned over his many transgressions, and the evil he had done to others. He alluded to the mysterious way he had been brought to see his wickedness and folly, but when he spoke of the love of God, through Christ, in pardoning his sins, he wept like a child. He concluded by declaring that he had enjoyed more real happiness in one hour since his conversion, than in all the time he was an infidel.

Many that were present were much affected, and wept tears of thankfulness for this additional evidence of the power of saving grace. One poor man, an old acquaintance of Emmott, declared that, "If he could be as happy as Dick Emmott, he would give all he had, even his donkey and cart."

My visit to Emmott after the public confession of his faith was to both of us a joyful meeting. He spoke of his deep confidence in God's mercy and love, and his firm conviction that He would sustain him amidst all the persecution and abuse he would probably have to suffer from his old companions. I then took up the Bible and, opening at the fifty-third of Isaiah, read—

"Surely He hath borne our griefs, and carried our sorrows: yet we did esteem Him stricken, smitten of God, and afflicted. But He was wounded for our transgressions, He was bruised for our iniquities: the chastisement of our peace was upon Him; and with *S*

His stripes we are healed. All we like sheep have gone astray; we have turned everyone to his own way; and the Lord hath laid on Him the iniquity of us all."

While reading this description of our Saviours suffering for us, tears streamed down Emmott's face. "What love! what love!" he exclaimed, "and all for guilty sinners—for such as me. O, what love!"

Emmott's prayer at parting was the simple, earnest breathing of a thankful heart.

"O Lord," said he, "how good Thou art! Never, never can I praise Thee enough for what Thou hast done for me. What a wicked, wicked man I have been, yet Thou, for Jesus Christ's sake, hast forgiven me. I know, I feel Thou hast. Christ did carry my griefs and sorrows; He was bruised for me, and by His stripes I am healed. Do help me to praise Thee! O do help me to praise Thee! and bless all my old companions. Open their dark eyes, and show them the Lamb of God, that taketh away the sin of the world. Do, Lord, do, for my dear Saviour's sake. Amen."

On parting, with a face beaming with joy, he said, "Do you know I am now admitted a member of the Church *1* Yes, I am; and now, living or dying, I have the unspeakable honour and pleasure of being a member of a Christian church. Happy day! happy day! who could have thought it!"

Yes, Emmott, who could have thought it! Let none despair, seeing that faith in Jesus can snatch from the very verge of hell, such a vile transgressor as the Oldham infidel—Richard Emmott. THERE is no doubt but that many women would be a vast deal better without husbands, than to Lave such wicked, miserable creatures as they are plagued with; and there is no doubt that many children would be great gainers by becoming fatherless, for they have fathers who are more to them a curse than a blessing. When I have witnessed the misery of some homes, and knew that it was caused by the conduct of those who ought to make these homes happy, I have thought that the best use we could make of some of our old coal-pits, would be to fill them with these torments, providing they had no souls, for they do not deserve either a coffin or a respectable grave. But this would not be Christianity. In this world we shall all

have something to exercise our charity and patience; and we are bound to do all we can to be a blessing to those who may be a curse to themselves. Instead of filling up old coal-pits with them, we must try to lead them to Him who died for the vilest of sinners.

But it is also true that many widows, like the widow mentioned in this narrative, are "widows indeed;" left like the sparrow on the house-top, aloue; bereaved of their stay and staff, forced to struggle with bitter adversity, and often to weep alone over their hapless condition. And it is a comfort to know that heaven has marked out the widow for its special care.

One of the noble replies given by Job to his "miserable comforters," when they charged him with having sent the widows empty away, was, that he had not turned a deaf ear to their cry, but had caused their "hearts to sing for joy." And one of the most touching scenes in the life of Peter, is when he stands looking at the dead body of Dorcas, and the weeping widows gather round to show him the garments she had made for them. One of the imperative orders given by the Almighty to the ancient Jews was, "Ye shall not afflict any widow, or fatherless child. If thou afflict them in any wise, and they cry at all unto me, I will surely hear their cry." And one of the standing tests of true religion before God is, that we "visit the fatherless and widows in their affliction."

There is a pleasing sketch, from the German, of a boy who saw his mother weeping, and, affectionately putting his arms round her neck, said, "Why do you weep, mother?" His mother replied,

"I did not know you saw my tears, my child. I have often wept in secret, for I did not want to make you sad by letting you see my sorrow; but since your father was taken away, I have found it hard work to provide you bread and pay your school fee. I intended to give you more learning before you began work, but I find I cannot; you will have to leave school, and help me to get food for yourself and two little sisters. I have got you the situation of an errand-boy, and you will have three shillings per

week."

"Well, don't weep, mother; I will be a good lad, and help you all I can," was the noble reply.,

The first day the little fellow went to his work, he was sent with letters to the post-office. He put them in one by one. The post-master stood at the door, and the lad very innocently said, "Where do all the letters that people put in your box go to *1*"

The post-master kindly explained to him, that if he wrote a letter, folded it up, sealed it, and wrote on the back the name and residence of the person he wished to receive it, it would go to him, wherever he lived.

That night the fatherless boy wrote the following letter:—

"To my Lord Jesus Christ in Heaven.

"My father is dead, and my mother weeps, and is sad because father is dead, and we are very poor. Mother wished to keep me to school a little longer, but she has no money; do help poor mother that she will not weep."

Having finished the letter, he folded it up, sealed it with some shoemaker's wax, wrote on the back: "To my Lord Jesus Christ in Heaven," and put it into the post-office.

When the post-master saw the letter, he could not tell what to do with it, and was holding it in his hand when a Moravian minister entered. He showed the minister the letter, observing,

"It is no use sending this to the dead letter-office; I will open it and return it to the simple person that has posted it, if I can find him out."

The letter was opened and read. The post-master and minister were much affected. The minister begged permission to read the letter at a Missionary meeting he was going to attend that evening. He read it to a large audience, and a lady rose exclaiming:

"Oh! that I knew the little boy that wrote that letter; he should go to school, and his mother and sisters should have bread."

The mother and child were both present. The mother held down her head in amazement and fear, for it was all new to her; but the little fellow, all exoitement, called out,

"Please, Ma'am, I am here!"

The good lady fulfilled her promise. The boy was gent to school again, and the widow found a friend in need.

Now, I ask, did not the contents of that letter go to heaven before the little boy posted it? I believe they did for God has given special promises to the orphan and widow. This little story is one illustration of the way in which He keeps these promises,—the following narrative is another.

In my seventh Report of the "Chapel for the Destitute," in the month of June, I mention having given relief to a widow. During the last winter I received a letter, asking if I should be at home the following evening, and stating that the writer was in trouble, and wished to see me on a very urgent matter. I replied that, having a published engagement in Stephenson-street Chapel, Manchester, I should not be at home, but might be seen on the day following.

I had forgot the stranger's letter until arriving at Stephenson-street, the Chapel-keeper informed me that i a lady was in the vestry, anxious to have an interview with me. On entering the vestry she rose, but was so agitated that I requested her to be seated, and to inform me, in as few words as possible, the nature of her errand, as the audience would soon be waiting. She tried to tell me, but was so fluttered and nervous that she could not proceed, for she evidently feared to mention the real object of her errand. My time having expired, I asked for her address, and promised to call as soon as possible.

On calling, according to promise, I found that the timid young woman I had seen on the previous evening, was the only child of an aged, respectable, and good-looking widow, keeping a small shop in Rochdale Road, Manchester. I was invited into the sitting room. The daughter entered with me; but both were so greatly embarrassed, that it was several minutes before the mother could inform me of their real object in wishing to see me. At length she said.

"Well, sir, I think I ought to apologise for giving you this trouble; and though

you have kindly fulfilled your promise in coming, I scarcely know how to begin. But if you will let me give you a little of my history, you will then better understand the request I have to make. Are you pressed for time *1* How long can you stay with us, sir?"

I looked at my watch, and replied, "About an hour-and a-half."

"Well, sir, I do not know what your first impressions about us are, but I have seen better days. I am of a good family, but my relations are all dead. I married a well-educated, gentlemanly man, a commercial traveller, representing what was thought to be a wealthy house. But the house failed, and for several months my husband was out of a situation. This took away most of our savings. He, however, got another place, and, when setting out on his first journey for the new house, he came to my bedside,—for I was then confined. Oh! how well I remember that morning. He had his overcoat and travelling rug on his ann; he looked cheerful, and affectionately bade me good morning. But in a few hours he was brought back—dead! He had just stepped on the steam packet, the boiler burst, and my dear Alfred was hurried into eternity!"

A fresh remembrance of the awfully sudden death of her husband brought a flood of tears to the eyes of the poor widow. She turned aside her head to hide them. For a moment we sat in silence. Thinking to direct the thoughts of the poor woman to what is of infinitely more importance than the death of the body, and having an impression that, in her case, joy would be mixed with grief, I observed,

"I do not think it is wrong to mourn over our departed loved ones. If we do not sorrow as those who have no hope, we have a bright spot in the cloud."

"Yes, sir, it is that which gives me the deepest pang, and makes my keenest sorrow. My Alfred was a scholar and a gentleman, but he was not a Christian. And, believing as I do, that as death leaves us, judgment will find us,—for our Saviour plainly tells us we must be born again, or we cannot see the kingdom of God,—believing this, and my

dear husband being cut off as he was,—almost killed me. For many, many days I refused to be comforted, for I feared that to him it was a double death. I had no bright spot in the cloud.

"But, once or twice, a little hope hovered over my mind. I then began to pray that the Lord would let the soul of my Alfred come back, to tell me if he was happy. For this I prayed incessantly. I refused to let my room be lighted in the night, expecting and believing he would be allowed to come back, and tell me he was saved. Every evening I tried to prepare my mind for the meeting, for I truly believed he was coming. And, at last, come he did! perhaps not really and truly, but to me it was really and truly,—call it a dream or what you will. He was dressed just as he was on the morning he came to my bedside to take leave of me, his overcoat and travelling rug on his arm. He looked me in the face, with a look of sorrow, and said, 'Sophia, you should not have done this. Why disturb me, why not submit to your fate! Your prayers and tears are of no avail for me now.'

"With a calmness, which now appears to me amazing, I answered, 'Alfred, my own dear Alfred, do tell me. Are you happy *1* Do tell me this, before you go back!'

"With the same look of sorrow, but in a lower and sadder voice, he replied, 'You know how I resisted the strivings of God's Spirit. I might have been saved. I have had ten thousand offers of mercy, and rejected them all. Farewell!'"

Here the mother paused, and for several minutes we again sat in silence; then turning to me she said,

"Mr. Ashworth,—do you know of any book that has been written with the object of giving comfort to those who are convinced they have dear friends or relatives in perdition?"

"No, I don't think such a book could be written. The Judge of all the earth will do right, and to believe that He will, is the only ground on which a smitten soul can find any repose. To believe that God is infinitely holy, and true, and righteous in His dealings with us, is the only thing that can teach such mourners as you to say 'Amen' to His mysterious doings."

"Yes, sir, I think you are right. Nevertheless it is very sad. I have often had a wish that I might be allowed to take my husband's place in hell, if he be there, providing his dear soul might go to heaven, for I could always better suffer myself, than see the sufferings of those I love."

"I don't think you are alone in that feeling," I replied; "but what did you do for bread after your husband's death ?"

"Well, sir, a very infirm relative, who was both able and willing to pay for being carefully nursed, hearing of my desolate condition, came to reside with me, and for several years I was able to keep on my house; but the relative dying, I, not being able to get another lodger, sold part of my furniture, and with the proceeds opened a small shop. For many years I worked hard, night and day, for a bare subsistence. Yet, careful as I was, I got a little in debt. To pay this off, I sold more furniture, and my husband's gold watch. About this time, the shop I occupied was sold, and my new landlord raised my rent so high that I could not possibly pay it. I removed to Rochdale Road, and again was nearly making bread, when the cotton famine almost destroyed my custom, and every month I found we were going down."

"Had my daughter's health been good, so that she could have learned some suitable business, perhaps we might have done better, but from a child she has been very delicate. A slight cold will confine her to bed for weeks; and the knowledge of her weak state, and our continual struggling to make ends meet, often makes her very dejected. We never have any of what are called luxuries. We live very cheaply and very bare, and perhaps this makes against the health of my child, but we must do so."

"And now, sir, I come to the part we wished to see you about. During the last seven years, we have lost ground by little and little, until I now owe two tradesmen more than I can pay. To some, what I owe would seem a mere trifle,

but to me it is a great sum. About six months since, I promised to pay them all on or before the 21st of June next, and have done all I can to fulfil my promise. The time is near at hand, and I shall not be able to keep my word. This greatly distresses me and my daughter. We have wept much and prayed much over the matter, for we believe in the goodness and providence of God, and trust we are both His spiritual children. If we are unable to keep on the shop, and our goods be taken, what shall we do? For, humanly speaking, we have not one relative or friend in this wide world to whom we could look for help."

"A few weeks since, I was reading your book Strange Tales from Humble Life,' and especially that narrative called, 'Twenty Pounds; or the Little Prayer.' While reading, I was astonished to find such a clear description of our own condition. After reading it, I said to my daughter,.' If there be help for us in this world, I have an impression it will come through the writer of this book.' We talked much about you, and earnestly sought for Divine guidance, and the result is the letter we sent you. I feel ashamed, and again make an apology for troubling you."

Having now become acquainted with the bereavements, trials, and struggles of the two truly respectable and, I thought, pious creatures, that sat in silence waiting my answer, I found it was my turn to become thoughtful. Eighteen pounds would pay all, and establish their credit with their tradesmen. The cotton famine was nearly over, and this sum might save two deserving creatures from misery and ruin. What shall I do? Yes, what shall I do? I have no eighteen pounds to spare. I have, every year, hundreds of cases of distress, but I relieve them with very small sums, and this sum would relieve many such cases. These were my thoughts, and, not knowing what to do, and fearing to crush all their hope, I at last said,

"Well, you must excuse my giving you no answer at present. I have a few wealthy friends, who might, if they knew of your case, give me something to help you. One of them has a long

knitted purse, one end of which, he says, specially belongs to the Lord, for He gives by rule, and gives much. Sometimes he tells me the Lord's end is getting rather full, and asks me if I have any real cases of need. I will see this good man, and ask him how his purse is, and let you know early."

With this promise they both seemed greatly satisfied, saying, that whoever found the money, they would gladly return it when able.

I saw my friend with the two-ended purse, but was sorry to find both ends just then were empty; but I was sure he had his own good reason for having given his all, for he gave much, and much comes to him to give.

T wrote to say that the purse was empty, but lest they should despair, promised to call and see them again.

On Sunday, the 18th of June, I had an engagement at York-street Chapel, Heywood. The day was very hot. Passing the house of one of my friends, residing betwixt Rochdale and Heywood, I called, requesting they would allow me to bathe my hands and face in cold water. I was shown upstairs into the bath-room. When I came down, the lady of the house said,

"Mr. Ashworth, I have just been reading to my husband your narrative of ' Twenty Pounds; or the Little Prayer,' and he thinks it was a very timely deliverance for old Mr. Gadsby, and so think I."

That moment a very strange sensation came over me, for I felt God was at work for the fatherless and widow.

"Indeed," I replied, "I have a little tale to tell yott about another person that has been reading that narrative;" and at once I told them all about the poor suffering creatures in Rochdale Road. They both heard me with the greatest interest, and one of them said,

"But surely you are not going to find them the money, are you?"

"I don't know that," I replied. "My Bible says, Blessed is he that considereth the poor, for the Lord will remember him in the time of trouble.' If I live, I, no doubt, shall have trouble. Yet it will be a great consolation to feel and know that the Lord will not forget me then."

For a moment both of them looked very thoughtful; and, my time having expired, I shook hands and left them.

On the morning of the 20th of June, I awoke much earlier than usual, for I had been much troubled in my sleep by, as distinctly as a dream can be distinct, seeing mother and daughter in greater trouble than ever. I at once saw I must immediately decide what to do, and I did determine to advance the eight pounds for one of the creditors, and see the other, and request him to wait another six months, and I would see that he did not lose his money. This I determined to do that day.

On opening my letters, on the morning I was going to see the distressed widow, one of them was from the house I had called at on the Sunday, and read as follows:— "dbabsie,

"After you left on Sunday, we could not help thinking of the two poor creatures you mentioned. It would be a very sad thing for them to be turned out of their living, and I write to say, we will furnish you with ten pounds. Will you be go kind as to convey it to them? The Lord bless you. "Yours truly,

On reading this letter, I thought,— Yes, God lives! He lives! He lives, and is a Father to the fatherless. A Judge to the widow is God in His holy habitation. Leave thy fatherless children and I will preserve them alive, and let thy widows trust in me. Yes, He lives, and blessed is the man that maketh the Lord his trust.

Some may say this was a singular chance or accident; a case of remarkable good luck. Indeed, people that believe in luck, chance, and accident, are very inconsistent, if they pray. Such persons heed not, or believe not, in an all-seeing, wise, and superintending Providence. A sparrow falls not to the ground without God's notice, and He tells His children, that the very hairs of their head are all numbered; and urges them to call on Him in the day of trouble, and He will deliver them. The doctrine of luck is the doctrine of the fatalist.

That day, on entering the little shop in Eochdale Road, the daughter was standing behind the counter, and seemed unusually calm; and I had an impression some one had been with help before me.

"Tou seem more cheerful to-day; have you got out of your difficulty VI asked,

"No, sir," was her reply. "I always feel happy when I see mother so. She is very much lifted-up with more than a conviction that we are to have help to-day." Then, with tears in her eyes, she said,

"I never saw my mother so earnest in prayer, and so long on her knees as she was last night. On rising she smiled at me, as I lay in bed, saying, 'Oh! how happy I feel! the Lord has really heard my prayer, and we shall see it very soon.'"

When the mother came into the shop, I laid the money down. She looked first at the money, then at her daughter, then at me; then folding her hands, she calmly said, "The Lord did not turn a deaf ear to the cry of the widow."

I left the little shop of the poor but now exceedingly happy mother and daughter, thankful that my Lord had honoured me by making me the medium through which He had sent help to His needy children, and wishing that the rich in this world's goods did but know how much real pleasure they forego by not honouring the Lord with their substance Many of them I know often feel the joys of doing good; and to do good is a real joy. These have the blessing of Him who has said, "Inasmuch as ye have done it to one of the least of these my brethren, ye have done it unto me. " And they will also have the blessing and the prayer of many a suffering one, many an orphan, and many a Widow. AN old Christian minister once called at my house, on returning from a visit to a member of his church. On sitting down, he for some time remained silent, gazing in the fire, then, lifting up his head, and looking me in the face, he said,—

"Oh dear! oh dear!-whatever must he done for the young women of our churches and schools, to prevent them making such miserable, wretched, ruin-ous marriages? I have just been to see one of our most promising young members, to inquire the reason of her long absence from the meeting, but I could get nothing from her but sobs and tears. Her mother, coming in at the time, informed me that the young man her daughter had married was very unsteady, and threatened to turn her out of doors if she attended chapel any more. 'But,' continued her mother, '*she said she would have him.*' Oh! that our young women were more cautious. What must be done for them? Can you tell V "Yes, I think I can," I replied. "The church and school must labour more earnestly to train up a better generation of young men for husbands; for husbands our young women *will* have, either good or bad."

The old minister, with a quiet smile, rose from his chair, put on his hat, took his crutch, and bade me good morning, but with a look that plainly told me he was sad at heart; for he was a good man, and mourned over this one stray sheep of his fold.

And what minister or Sunday school teacher, that has been long in the work, and who has cared for the future of our young females, has not often had to pass through the same painful experience 1 I have had many a foolish wish in my time, but I think one ofthe most foolish was one Sunday, when speaking to about two thousand young men and women, I then felt a desire to see what would be their ultimate destiny. I believed, and told them, that the joys and sorrows of this world and the next greatly depended on the characters they were then forming, and the company they were keeping, especially in relation to marriage. Oh! what havoc being unequally yoked has made,—what wretched homes,—what blighted hopes,—what broken hearts,—what early graves!

The case of the young wife mentioned by the old minister I knew something of at the time, and have seen many more such cases since; and thinking one of them may serve to check others who are near the same brink of ruin, I give it to warn my young female friends to be wise in time.

I distinctly remember that, about ten o'clock one Sunday morning, I was standing at the desk in one of our schools, looking with pleasure on the teachers and scholars as they all seemed cheerfully engaged in their various places. A fellow-teacher who was also looking on the pleasing scene, smilingly observed,—

"How happy they look, especially the young women in the Bible class. I wish they may never be less joyous than they are just now."

Sarah, the subject of this narrative, was one of the happy ones who sat amongst the Bible scholars that morning, and, I believe, loved the school with an affection as deep as any then present. She could read and sing well, had a cheerful, open countenance, and, being full of life and spirit, contributed to the pleasures of those around her. But she had one failing, the consequences of which she did not then see,—she was fond of Sunday evening walks, and sometimes these walks were not in the best company. It was in one of these Sunday evening walks that she met with the young man who afterwards became her husband; and, as good Christian young men are not found lounging or strolling through streets, lanes, or fields on the Sabbath, we may fairly conclude that Sarah was now in great danger; for, of all the important periods of a young woman's life, there are none more momentous than those hours in which she first listens to the soft declarations of a young man. Oh! how much of weal or woe depends on that moment! Yet by thousands of young women that moment is never seriously considered.

Stephen, the young man who had confessed his love to Sarah, was a bold, swaggering fellow, who boasted he could go to church, say "amen," dance a jig, swear an oath, and drink a glass of ale. He worked at the milk got tolerable wages, and was of a poor but respectable family. In choosing a wife, he did not consider it necessary to consult either his own parents or the parents of his intended, and Sarah, in this respect, was too much like him. Forgetting, or deceiving the guide of her youth, she kept it a secret from those that loved her most, and would probably have guided her best. In this respect they both dishonoured their parents, and God's blessing never yet rested on such, and never will.

The consequence was, that when Stephen went to visit Sarah, he went late, or in the dark, and whistled once, twice, or three times, as had been agreed upon. She then made soma excuse for going out, and walked with him in bye-ways, sly-ways, and dark-ways, forgetting that no young man, worth a straw, ever thought better of any young woman for so far losing her self-respect as to walk with him in sly-ways. To both of them it is low and degrading, and to one of them it often proves worse than death.

When it became known that Sarah was keeping company with Stephen, many of the more serious scholars, and several of her fellow-teachers (for she had now become a teacher) warned her of the consequences. They told her he had often been seen drunk, and that he attended no place of worship; and the dear old creature who had been, if possible, more than a mother, besought her to give him up, and be warned in time. One evening, when they were more earnestly urging this upon her, she replied,—

"When we get married I think he will mend; but, say what you will, and do what you will, *I will have*

After this her friends gave up the struggle, and ceased to speak to her on the subject. She was left to take her own course, and in a few months after she was married. In a short time after, her new husband came home one evening, to use his own expression, "As drunk as a lord."

That was a bitter evening to Sarah. She wept most of the night, and the following day, when he was sober, she besought him never to enter a public house again. But he doggedly replied,—

"I like a pint of ale, and I shall have one when I think proper, and shall not be talked to by anybody. You knew it before you had me. Tou made your bar-gain with your eyes wide open."

Whether Sarah's eyes were opened before her marriage to Stephen, admits of some doubt, but now they were being opened with a vengeance. She became very dejected, and wished to tell her troubles to her former friends, but durst not, knowing they had done all they could to prevent the very thing now come to pass. For fifteen years she had been in connexion with the school and church, and, being a member, she had attended many prayer meetings, and once or twice had engaged in prayer; but from the time she began to keep company with Stephen, her conscience had been ill at ease, she had neglected to pray, and absented herself from the means of grace when she could have attended. But now her burdened soul had nowhere else to go but to Him whose guidance she had failed to ask, and who would have directed her steps, had she asked in time.

Stephen grew worse and worse. Saturday and Sunday nights were spent in the public house. Stronger and stronger became his desire for drink. He neglected his work, got discharged, and, to hide their disgrace and shame, they left that neighbourhood, and came to reside in Rochdale. But he did not leave behind him his drunken habits, and the result was, that husband and wife, and their two small children, were all clothed in rags. Indeed, so reduced were they that Sarah pawned her last remaining property, her precious Bible, for six-pence, to buy her children bread!

It was about this time she came to my office. Her eyes were red with weeping, and, in great earnestness, she besought me to try to find her husband employment, and do what I could to induce him to give up drinking. She persuaded him to come and see me, and he then promised he would reform his life, keep to work, and be better to his family. For several weeks he kept to his promise, and came with his wife every Sunday to the Chapel for the Destitute. Sarah, poor thing, was quite overjoyed at the change. She became better dressed, and smiles were again lighting up her sorrow-smitten countenance. From a child she had been a good singer, and often her clear, full voice,—while chanting sweet melodies, dear to her in her earlier, happier days,—rose in fine tones above the whole of our congregation. She sang,—and wept for joy as she sang,—the sweet songs of praise to Him who seemed again nearer and dearer to her now lightened and comparatively happy soul.

Oh! ye young, happy wives,—whose sober, loving husbands sing, and sit, and kneel with you in the blessed house of prayer,—whose mingled devotions ascend from peaceful hearts to fill with incense those golden vials before the heavenly throne,—oh! breathe a prayer for such as Sarah, whose soul is filled with joy, because she shares with you but one short month of wedded happiness.

The gathering cloud was again casting its dark shadow over Sarah's path. She had rejoiced with trembling, knowing how weak are the best resolves of the prayerless,—for Stephen was a prayerless man. One morning, when going to his work, he met two of his old pot companions, who jeered him about going to chapel. Stephen was like thousands such weak men, he could better stand a blow in the face, or a thump in the ribs, than the finger of scorn. Gibes and sneers were stronger than his love for his wife, his children, his God, or his soul. He winced and shamed, and, to show them he was a man, went with them into a public house.

That day I received the following letter,—

"Sir,—Will you send me three shillings by the man that brings this note? My husband is so ill I cannot leave him. Do send me three shillings. Yours,

"SARAH."

I read the note, and, looking at the man that brought it, said,—

"Well, old fox, you have planned this well; but if Stephen and you had what many better men have had, you would have a rope tied round both your necks, and be hanged up, back to back."

The idle drunkard sneaked out of my office as fast as possible. He was one

of the two men who had that morning sneered at, and entrapped foolish Stephen. I knew the man, and had often tried to do him good. He had attended the Chapel for the Destitute several times, and promised fair for becoming a changed character; but one Sunday morning I found him helplessly drunk, under the windows of an empty house. The water from the drop-spout was pouring over him, and he looked like a drowned dog. I pulled him from under the water-spout, and gave him a good shake. He opened his eyes, stared me in the face, and, seeing who it was, said,—

"Is that you, Mr. Ashworth i Ah man! you tried to convert me, but you could not. I am above your cut; yes, I am above your cut."

I felt distressed that the man should think I had power to convert. None can do that but God.

About two hours after the man had called with the note I met Sarah. I had the note in my pocket, and showed it to her. I shall not soon forget her look of agony; I expected every moment she would fall to the ground. Her anguish was such that she could not speak,—she put both hands to her breast, to hold her throbbing heart. Pale as death, and without saying a word, she turned back, and went to seek her miserable husband, who, she fondly thought, was comfortably at work. Poor creature! what a picture of misery and despair.

Stephen was degraded enough before this last fall, but after this he became more and more debased. Drunkenness and idleness often go together, and Stephen's conduct became so bad that no one, who knew him, would employ him. He began to associate with the worst rabble in the town, and lost all regard for his sorrowing wife and two helpless children. Sarah got a little charing and washing, when she could, but she, too, sank lower and lower every day. The little furniture they had was sold for debt, and they were compelled to take shelter in a very poor lodging-house. Her friends helped her a little, when they could do it unknown to her husband, and had she been a widow, she would have been much better assisted;

for those that wish to help a drunkard's wife fear to do so, and the poor creature is worse than a widow. A drunkard's wife is doubly cursed.

On going to my office one morning, I found Sarah standing in the passage, waiting to see me. She tried hard to tell me her errand without weeping, but her pent-up feelings burst forth in a flood of tears. After being thus relieved, she said,—

"I have come to tell you that Stephen is a little steadier just now, and he says he will try to do something to get a little bread for us. He knows that no one will employ him, but he thinks that if he could get a barrow and go out hawking, he could make a little money."

"What does he think of hawking?" I asked.

"Cockles and mussels," she replied.

"How will he get them?"

"Well, sir, I have come to ask you to lend me six shillings to buy them with. I will pay you back at the rate of sixpence per week."

"But you know, Sarah, that if Stephen gets any money he will drink it, and then how can you get a fresh stock of cockles and mussels."

"Yes, I know he will, if left to himself; but I will go with him, and draw all the money."

A few evenings after Sarah had been in my office, I was coming through a village, outside the town, and heard Stephen crying " Cockles and mussels, alive O!" and saw Sarah walking by the barrow to draw the money. I crossed the street lest she should see me, for I wished to spare her feelings, but could not help thinking of the time when I saw her in the Sunday school, a well-dressed, happy, cheerful young woman, and contrasting it with her present condition. Then, full of hope and promise; now, a poor, ragged, sorrow-smitten creature, shivering in the streets, with her drunken, idle husband, shouting "Cockles and mussels!" And I also remembered that she said, when warned by her friends, *"I will have him I"*

Oh! I wish our young women would take warning from the many sad examples, to be seen every day, of the untold misery arising from thoughtless marriages What a blessing it would be if every young woman would ask herself the following questions when a young man first speaks to her:—" Is he good to his parents? Does he swear 1 Does he go into a public house? What sort of company does he keep? Does he regularly attend a place of worship?" Depend upon it, if he be not good to his parents, if he takes God's name in vain, goes into public houses, keeps bad or doubtful company, and attends no place of worship, the woman will be a fool that expects to be anything but miserable with such a man. Nor is it suprising if such, like Sarah, should have to cry "Cockles and mussels!"

The little improvement that had taken place in Stephen enabled them to get a poor second-hand bed and an old table, and with these they removed into a cellar. The elder boy was getting two shillings and sixpence per week, but the younger was running ragged and wild about the streets; for Stephen, like many drunken parents, would not deprive himself of one pint of beer to get his child to school. Seeing the little, miserable boy in the streets, and knowing that, like thousands of such, the fault was not his own, I gave him a note to the teacher of Sparrow-hill School, promising that, if he would take the boy, I would pay his school fee. The little fellow took the note, was admitted, and, a few days after, he gave me such a smile as well paid me for all I had done for him. A smile from a drunkard's child is worth something.

Sarah's health failing her a little, she was unable to go out with Stephen, and the consequence was what she expected,—he drank the money with which he ought to have purchased a fresh stock, and became worse than ever; for, like many drunkards, though he brought nothing home, he abused his wife if she did not find him sufficient food.

One Saturday evening Sarah came to my house. On going to the door to ask her errand, I found she had brought with her their oldest child, a boy about eleven years of age. She told me he had only part of one shirt, and that she had

to wash it after he had gone to bed. I promised the little fellow a shirt, for I well remembered how I myself had many times gone to bed on the Saturday evening while my poor mother washed and mended mine. I noticed, while Sarah was speaking to me, that she covered one side of her face with her apron, but though she tried to hide it, I saw that one of her eyes was very much swollen and quite black.

"What is the matter with your face, Sarah? How is it your eye is so black 1" I inquired.

Sarah began weeping, which soon caused the little fellow to weep also. She told me that her husband had been doing a little work, for which he was to have four shillings; that she had gone to the person he was working for to borrow two shillings, to get a little bread for herself and children; and that when Stephen found he had only two shillings for drink, he came home and almost killed her.

Several months after this, late one evening, after she had put the two boys to bed, and got as good a supper as she could for her husband, she sat on the bed-side, the only seat in the house, and was reading a Bible she had borrowed from a neighbour. The moment Stephen came in, he looked at his supper, and, fixing his eyes on her, growled out, "Is that all?"—then with a deep oath he swore he would chop her head off. He then kicked the table over, rolled into bed beside his trembling children, without taking off his dirty clothes, and soon fell fast asleep!

His terrible look, and more terrible threat, so greatly frightened Sarah that she durst scarcely remain in the house. All night she sat in the corner in great fear. She durst not fall asleep, or make the least noise, and if he moved she trembled from head to foot. Oh! how she prayed that God would not forsake her, but help and protect her in this dreadful hour!

The fearful mental sufferings of that dreadful night had such an effect upon Sarah that she lost all spirit, for she daily expected her husband would murder her. So completely was she crushed by

continual bad treatment and suffering, that one evening, or rather about two in the morning, she leaped from her miserable bed, tore off her ragged night cap, opened the door, and, with nothing on but her night-dress, ran down the Foundry Brow, her hair flying loose behind as she ran, till she came to the end of Water 60 SARAH; OR, "I WILL HAVE HIM."

Street. She then stood still, and, looking up at the bright, full moon, she lifted up her right hand, and in a clear, full voice sang—yes, the poor, stricken creature *sang,*—and she sung one of those sweet. hymns she had often sung when happy in the Sabbath school. That sweet hymn was,—

"When I can read my title clear To mansions in the skies,
I'll hid farewell to every fear,
And wipe my weeping eyes.

There shall I bathe my weary soul In seas of heavenly rest,
And not a wave of trouble roll
Across my peaceful breast."

She sung only the first and last verses, but how fully the words expressed her condition!

The wild, warbling tones of a female voice, in the dead of night, woke many of the surrounding sleepers, who, filled with wonder, opened their windows, and looked out on the strange, astonishing scene. The police stood in amazement, but one of them took her by the hand, and, knowing where she lived, kindly took her home. She went with him, quiet as a child. Sarah, poor Sarah! had lost her reason. A cruel, idle, drunken husband had driven her mad.

But she said to her kind friends, who warned her in time, "Say what you will, and do what you will,
I WILL HAVE HIM!" r' there be, in this wide. wide world, one spot more calculated than another to roll back turbulent emotions, tame ambitious aspirations, and bring down lofty pretensions, it is the bed of long, lingering, protracted sickness. There the true value of things is tested, and the discovery made of what only can be trusted. The gilding and the tinsel fade away before the real and the substantial; for there we view

objects through a sober medium. And if there be a place, under heaven, from which can be gathered evidence the most convincing, and testimony the most enduring, of what saving faith can do, it is those same secluded, and often obscure chambers, where wearisome days and nights are appointed, for weeks, months, and years.

Oh, it is easy in life's tranquil day,

When all around is peace, to kneel and say,

"Father, Thy will be done!" But when that Will

Calls us to suffer, and be patient still,—

When God's mysterious ways are yet unknown,

When clouds and darkness veil His awful throne,

How then we need His all-supporting hand,

To bow submissive to the high command,—

To trust Him still in life's be-clouded day,

In resignation meekly then to say,

"Thy will be done!"

Yet this has been done myriads of times since that gloomy night when our Saviour said it, while sweating great drops of blood.

Perhaps few men living can reckon amongst their acquaintances such a variety of character as I can, and fewer still have the unspeakable privilege of communing with so many remarkable illustrations of the sustaining power of religion in almost every condition of life, but more especially during long and painful bodily affliction. Two of these I have already recorded in "Priscilla" and "Trials," others still remain, several of whom constitute the chief subject of the following sketches.

MARY.

In a comparatively quiet street, not far from the Ieeds Town Hall, in a small but neat chamber, may be seen one of my many sick friends. Judging from her letters, her choice selection of books, and her keen perception of the pure and beautiful in language, poetry, and flowers, she must have had some one to care for her in her early days. She belongs to the Society of Friends, and I first heard of her while staying at the house of Mr. John Whiting, Moreland Terrace, also one of the Friends. I was introduced to her by a young friend, who, on entering the room, took hold of the invalid's hand, saying,

"How art thou to-day, Mary? I think thou looks nicely. I have brought with me one whom I think thou wilt be glad to meet, and who wishes to see thee."

A slight flush came over her placid countenance, but with a quiet smile she replied,

"I have much to be grateful for, and I thank thee for thy kindness in remembering me, and bringing John Ashworth with thee." Then looking to where I stood, she held out her hand, saying, "Thou art come to see a poor creature, but I make thee very welcome. Wilt thou take a chair, for I want to talk with thee about thy poor people, and thy labours amongst them."

Interviews betwixt kindred spirits are amongst the sweetest joys of earth. Relationships, pure and strong, often arise from sympathy of views and feelings. Several years have rolled away since this our first meeting, and have made me more acquainted with Mary's character and history, but only confirming my first impression, that this daughter of suffering was a child of God, an heir of heaven.

"I thank thee for thy kindness in remembering me," was her feeling expression to the young guide that first led me to her sick chamber. No doubt many had long forgotten her, and many more, since the day she found herself a helpless invalid, had passed away. Some that had smoothed her pillow, shared her sorrows, and wiped her falling tears, had gone to brighter climes, leaving their afflicted one still in the wilderness. Farewells and parting scenes are amongst the sad way-marks through life; and on them, though sad, the memory often lingers longest, recalling again and again the looks, words, smiles, and tears,—the hopes, joys, and sorrows of the loved ones gone before. And the more of those loved ones pass before us through the gates of paradise, the near-er paradise seems to us, and the pain of parting is almost lost by the sweet thought of again uniting.

A mongst the felicities of this life, the bright scenes of this world, is an unbroken, happy family. And such was once the family of my sick friend,—all there, all round the hearth and the altar, when her health began to fail. The mother was taken first; three months after the father lost all his property, but not his character; four months after her sister died, saying with her last breath, "If God will permit me, I will come back and be your guardian angel." A family of nine became reduced to three,—the father, a sister, and my sick friend. For ten years this sister, night and day, watched over the afflicted one; then her summons came. In her last hours she begged to be laid beside her she had so long and tenderly nursed, and there, in the same bed, lying by her side, she breathed her last. For a short time her dear father was spared to her. But one evening he entered her room, his countenance radiant with joy, to inform his sick child of a cheering discourse delivered in the Meeting House that day, on the blessedness of the heavenly city. After sitting some time, he took a more than usually affectionate leave. In the morning he was found dead in bed!

How dreary, dark, and desolate must Mary's lot now appear to those whose Christian experience has never sounded those deeper depths of God's mysterious providence! Die we must, and it matters little how, or when, or where, if we die well. It is far more comforting to know that our dear relatives and friends are safely anchored in heaven's harbour, than to be daily fearing they will be wrecked on the shoals of perdition. When heaven calls the Christian home,

It is the voice that Jesus sends
To call them to His arms.

Mary knew this, and through her tears could say, "It is the Lord; let Him do what seemeth Him good;" for, in one of her letters to me, she says,

"When our heavenly Father puts His dear children into the fiery furnace, He sits by to conduct the needful refining process, and will, in His own time,—

which is ever the best time,—bid them come forth purified. People of the world count it all joy when they are in ease and affluence, but the real Christian is taught to count it all joy when he is tried as gold in the fire, for—

"He knows how much the weak can bear, And helps them when they cry;
The strongest have no strength to spare,
  For such He'll strongly try."

Mary's letter may seem to the worldling very melancholy, but let the worldling remember that one drop of the Atlantic bears a greater proportion to that ocean than time bears to eternity. A child of God may have, on one hand, "affliction for a moment," but he has, on the other, "a far more exceeding and eternal weight of glory." The darkest day of the Christian is streaked with light, more precious than the brightest day of the sinner. Of this, Mary is only one of thousands of witnesses; but she *is* one, for there are few happier creatures this side heaven. And part of that happiness consists in recognising the hand of God in everything, in being calm and cheerful, never idle, doing all the good she can by caring for others. Though utterly unable to move her body, she often employs her mind and hands in writing, reading, sewing, knitting, and working useful articles. I was much pleased with the neatness and orderly arrangement of Mary's sick chamber, and saw how attention to a few little matters greatly contributed to her comfort. Her canary, singing his sweet songs, going in and out of his cage at pleasure, often alighting on her finger to beg a crumb of bread, had been her cheerful companion for eight years. She had small flower-pots with choice plants,—a little mahogany and glazed library of well-selected books, so close to her bed, that she could reach the volume she wanted,—and a small writing case, containing all she required for recording her thoughts or conducting her correspondence.

But what surprised me most was her book-stall. On a stand beside her bed there was a square box with a glass cover. In this box she had several shillings' worth of small religious works, ranging in price from threepence to tenpence. These «he had bought at the wholesale price, and was selling them to her visitors retail, and all the profits went to relieve a very poor, afflicted creature, residing in the neighbourhood. Mary had heard of her sad condition, and, wishing to send her a little help, had established her book-stall to provide her with means, for which the poor creature was very thankful. When I first saw this book-stall, and learned the purpose for which it was opened, I thought that Mary, in her weakness and helpless affliction, was doing more on her sick bed for the glory of God, and the poor and needy, than thousands who were blessed with unbroken health and ample means. I believe Mary has a strong desire to do all the good she can,— her sympathies are very wide. I have received from her, as a present for my poor people of the "Destitute," a beautiful complete needle-case in silk, with pattern in white beads, her own working, which sold for fifteen shillings.
It is now thirty years since Mary sickened and lay down in the bed from which she has never been able to rise. During those thirty years, dear relatives and friends have passed away. A kind and affectionate servant, who has been long in the family, is all that now remains of a once numerous household. If the honest doubter respecting the truths of Christianity longs to be convinced,— if the formalist in religion wishes to see the power of real saving grace,—if the timid Christian desires to know if strength will be given according to the day,—if the long-tried child of God mournfully asks, "Can and will He still sustain me in these my heavy sorrows *1*"—and if the minister of the gospel wants powerful evidence of what faith in Christ can do in upholding, cheering, blessing, and sustaining through thirty years of bereavements, affliction, and pain, let them see this monument of triumph and victory.

I now take leave of Mary, more than ever persuaded that religion is the pearl of great price, the one thing needful.
ANOTHER MARY.
Before leaving Leeds I will again call

to see another of my sick friends, residing in a neat cottage near Brunswick Chapel. She, too, is called Mary.

I have often thought that the busy, bustling crowds, passing too and fro through the noisy streets of our towns and cities, little know how frequently they are very near to sights and scenes vastly different from the dazzle and show presented by trade and commerce, carriages, shops, and fashions, hearty laughter and merry greeting. The lowered blinds and closed shutters tell us when the dead are near, but how many chambers there are where the last foe is just entering, with short warning; how many where the soft tread and faint whisper tell of feeble frames and anxious thoughts; and how many on the couch and the bed are doomed to the feebleness of old age, or chained by chronio disease, as with bars of iron! This last is the condition of our sick friend near Brunswick Chapel.

This sufferer, in her younger years, was in business and it was while serving in the shop that she caught a cold, followed by a severe illness, which terminated in the stiffening of every joint, and deprived her of all power to move hand or foot. During this time she not only lost all the hard-earned savings of many years, and became absolutely penniless, but was in debt to tradesmen with whom she had done business. This greatly distressed her, and, out of the money contributed by friends for her sustenance, she managed, in ten or twelve years, by denying herself everything save the barest necessaries, to scrape together a sum sufficient to pay all her debts! Her thoughtfulness and kindness for those who suffer is most remarkable, and many deserving cases have, by her instrumentality, been brought under the notice of those who are able and willing to relieve the poor and distressed.

On my first visit to this patient sufferer, she expressed her great pleasure in seeing me, and I felt thankful that anything I had written had been made to her a blessing, or had given her one moment's comfort. She spoke of "Priscilla" and "Trials" as having greatly strengthened her faith, and brightened her hopes, and, with deep emotion, offered up a prayer on my behalf, that God would still keep me in my labours amongst the poor, the sick, and the afflicted.

She has several kind friends who almost daily call upon her. One benevolent gentleman has paid her rent for seventeen years, and frequently calls to converse with her. Another gentleman has his regular periods of calling, and spends much time in storing her mind with the precious promises of God's word; and a Christian lady often calls to read to her the Lessons and Prayers of the day. These are to Mary friends indeed, and she cannot speak of their kindness without weeping.

Oh, how rich and joyous are the pleasures of doing good. How sweet the thought that we can, in any measure, mitigate human woe, or increase, in the smallest degree, the happiness of one suffering fellowcreature. If, by a look, a smile, or a word, we can stay the falling tear,—if, by giving a little of our abundance, we lessen the anxieties of indigence, producing gladness, where otherwise there would be sadness, surely angels must covet such a privilege. The sordid, selfish man knows nothing of this. He may have mountains of gold, and millions of acres, and be clothed in purple and fine linen, and fare sumptuously every day, but there is a worm at his heart, a pang in his conscience; for only they that *do* good can ever *enjoy* good. Only they whose souls are moved with sympathy can know the higher states of human felicity. And how much do such as Mary stand in need of our commiseration!

It is hardly possible for the healthy and strong to form any adequate conception of the truly helpless condition of Mary, who for twenty-eight years has lain in her present deplorable state without power to move, and entirely dependent on others even for a drop of water. And yet she is made happy by the sweet presence of her Saviour, the deep consolations of religion, the glorious prospects of an eternal home amongst those that are clothed in white robes,

and have come out of great tribulation.

This home in heaven, as the sufferer lies

On her bed of pain, and uplifts her eyes
To that bright world, what a joy is given
By the blessed thought of a home in heaven l

Yes, Mary is happy, amidst loneliness, helplessness, and dependence, reaching over the long period of twenty-eight years. Her redeemed soul basks in celestial sunshine, lighting up her countenance with holy rapture, teaching all around her the unspeakable happiness of being a child of God, and possessing what the world can neither give nor take away.

We now take our leave of Mary, to call on another of my sick friends, who also resides in Yorkshire.

AGNES.

Those who have stood on the top of Castleberg Bock, overlooking the little, quiet, respectable town of Settle, in Yorkshire, will see, stretching out for many miles, some of the finest grazing ground in the world. The farmsteads, dotting these rich pasture-lands, seem from a distance to be homes of peace and plenty; and the inhabitants of the miniature city, at the foot of the rock, carry on their commercial pursuits without the breathless race for riches that characterizes the residents of our large towns. Here the excited London, Liverpool, or Manchester tradesman would be likely to go mad, for the prospect of becoming immediately rich would be cut *off.* To him Settle would be almost as lonely as the silent cities of Idumea. But perhaps his greatest surprise would be, that he had time to think of his eternal prospects, and on the short span of his present existence.

In the month of February, while carefully descending the rock, in the company of my host, Mr. Tatham, we were surprised to see, amidst the frost and snow, a wall-flower in full bloom. Mr. Tatham plucked the flower, saying, "The winter's storms have not killed thee, thou pretty little thing!" How it was I know not, but the sight of that flower drew my thought to an inhabitant of one of the small cottages at the foot

of the rock. Flowers are all beautiful, especially winter flowers, but in that cottage there was something more beautiful,—a meek, patient, suffering Christian, who, for many winters, had bloomed amidst the chilling, blasting winds of bereavement, sickness, and poverty.

My visit to this remarkably small, but pleasingly neat cottage, constitutes one of the way-marks of my life; for here I learned another lesson that taught me how often I had been unthankful for mercies, and forgetful of the goodness and providence of God. To many, the sickness of a few days, a week, or a month, is a terrible trial for their patience, and a cause of much fretfulness and murmuring; but here years may be counted since Agnes was smitten with weakness of the spine. Yet there she still lies, the helpless victim of this terrible stroke.

Sometime after Agnes began to be sick, her mother became unable to leave her bed. For three years they lay in two small separate rooms,—Agnes upstairs, and the mother below,—and, for the whole of that time, they never saw each other. Both were so helpless that neither could move. When the mother was laid in her coffin, that coffin was brought to the bedside of the bereaved child, that she might lay her clammy hand on the parent's cold forehead, before she was carried to her silent home. Agnes often speaks of this as her greatest trial, but the thought of a mother in heaven is not a mourning without hope.

To be sick and penniless,—to subsist on the small pittance allowed by the town,—to depend upon others for a place where the weary may lay their head,—to be only able to speak in a whisper,—to be shut out from the busy world by day, and often to lie sleepless and restless in the night,— to endure pain of body and weariness of mind, without the faintest hope of ever having relief, till the stricken form shall be laid in the dust, is the sad, sad lot of poor Agnes Cooper. How often would the crumbs that fall from the rich man's table be to such an unspeakable blessing! And we are glad to know that a few such crumbs have found their way to her feeble hands, yielding the rich reward of the falling tear of thankfulness. By the kindness of a wealthy Friend, residing at Stratford-on-Avon, I have been provided with special means for special cases, and Agnes has not been forgotten. When handing to her the small portion allotted, her face first became red, then white; tears shot from her eyes, and, speechless with joy, she pointed to the spot where she wished me to kneel and join her in thankfulness to Him who had raised up for her this unknown friend. It was a moment of unspeakable bliss. Would that the donor had been there to witness it! But He who was the real Giver would see and record this gratitude from His suffering child.

Yes, Agnes, like the two Marys of Leeds, is one of the Lord's precious jewels, and she, like them, knew the real source of her deepest and firmest comfort. In her last letter she writes,—

"I am now thirty years old, and it is near fifteen years since my feeble form sank beneath the stroke; but I think that it is somehow all for the best, though I cannot now understand it, and it is sometimes hard to say, 'Thy will be done!' The last fortnight I have been so happy, both night and day; the sweet promises of the Saviour have been more than ever precious. I have been forced to cry out, 'Bless the Lord, O! my soul, and forget not all His benefits.' Oh, I feel I can trust Him to the end.

"For what are all my sufferings here,
If, Lord, thou count me meet,
With the enraptured host to appear,
And worship at Thy feet I
"Give joy or grief, give ease or pain,
Take life or friends away,
I soon shall meet them all again,
In that eternal day.

"Oh! to be present with the Lord, where there is no poverty, pain, or tears,—where the inhabitants never say they are sick. What a glorious prospect! And this prospect, through Him that washed me from my sins in His own blood, is mine;—yes, it is mine!"

We now take our leave of Agnes. Like Mary, she has chosen the good part. In her distress she sought and found the Lord, and in the little cottage at the foot of Castleberg Rock there is another witness That RELIGION IS AN EVERGREEN.

ANN. NO doubt there are many persons still living who can remember this world before it was turned downside up;—when men made their wills, appointed executors, and in tears bid adieu to dear friends, when setting out from our provincial towns to London, by the amazingly rapid coach the "Highflier," performing the journey in three days, "God willing." Then, packhorses plied betwixt market towns, bearing on their backs the merchandise of counties; and the poor tradesman thought it something grand to put on his great coat and muffler, wrap straw bands round his legs and feet, and mount the grocer's cart at midnight, to get to the nearest market by day-break in the morning. And when that wonderful and daring innovation on good old customs, the *canal,* was first opened, people cried shame on the companies for cutting up good land, declared they would never venture their lives in such a dangerous mode of journeying, and wondered what next they would live to see.

I have not seen much of these old-world views, for they were dissolving, and other scenes appearing, when I first began to look around me. But I well remember once paying my fare at Lancaster to go down (or up) to Kendal by a two-horse packet boat; and I also remember a loving old couple at the starting place greatly perplexing each other. The husband was urging his wife to venture on board the vessel, thinking there was not much danger, and she was beseeching him to walk for greater safety. Not being able to persuade him, she timidly came on deck, saying,—

"Well, I will go if thou goes; for if thou art drowned I might as well be drowned too."

It was while on this journey, from Lancaster to Kendal, that I heard two old men talking about one of their neighbours, who had been long lying on a sick-bed, and expressing a hope she might soon be released. They called her Ann.

It was more than twenty years after this, my first visit to Kendal, that I received an urgent request to speak at a public meeting on behalf of a society, having for its object the visiting and relieving the indigent sick and poor of that town. On my arrival I was informed by Mr. Gaskell, one of the oldest workers in this truly Christian labour, that a person who had been long afflicted was very anxious I should call and see her. On hearing the name, I was astonished to find that it was the same I had heard the two old men conversing about on the boat, and I at once promised to pay her a visit as soon as possible.

Those who have travelled through this stone-built town, bordering the lake district of Westmoreland, will have observed that, like many ancient places, it principally consists of one long, wide street, out of which run numerous courts or narrow openings, leading to groups of buildings occupied by many of the inhabitants. It was up one of these courts, in Strickland Grate, where the invalid I was requested to see resided, and I was pleased with the neat and comfortable appearance of many of the small whitewashed dwellings, particularly the one we entered. I am always glad to see clean, happy looking cottage homes, especially amongst professors of religion; for I do not believe in a dirty Christianity. And the whitened door step, the well rubbed oak stairs, and the orderly little back chamber in which lay my sick friend, all told of a careful, thoughtful nurse, whom I afterwards found to be, what I at first suspected, a kind, patient Christian, greatly respected by all, and much beloved by her who had been so long the object of her care.

My first interview with Ann was one of sadness, mingled with much pleasure. I could not but remember the long, long time she had been lying feeble and almost helpless; that one generation had passed away and another had come since that fearful accident, which resulted in this lingering weakness. But when I saw her cheerful, happy looking countenance, and heard her tell of the deep settled peace she constantly enjoyed, springing from union and communion with the Saviour, my concern for her body was lost, in sharing the joys of her soul.

The accident referred to above, and which nearly proved fatal on the spot, took place on Mint Bridge, about one mile from Kendal. Ann, with several others, had been out in a conveyance. On returning, from some cause, it was upset; her head was dashed against the stones, and the conveyance fell on her body. She was carried home unconscious, having received inp juries from which nothing short of a miracle could ever restore her. She was then about seventeen years of age, and had lost her father five years previous to the accident. Before he died, he affectionately enjoined upon Ann his desire that she would still attend the place of worship with her mother, until she was able to judge for herself. Her mother died six years after, committing her child to the care of Him who is the Father of the fatherless. The few pounds left by the mother was well husbanded by Ann's nurse, every penny spent being carefully entered in a book, until the last penny was gone.

And now came a severe trial of Ann's faith; she was reluctant to receive parish relief, knowing how very poor many were who had to pay the rates. She prayed earnestly for many weeks that the Lord would some way send her deliverance from this sore trouble. One day a Christian lady, calling to see her, left a sovereign on her bed, and soon after she received five pounds through the post. She was overwhelmed with joy, for she considered these gifts as from the skies, and at once declined to receive any further aid from the town.

Another test and painful trial of her faith was permitted, one that almost caused her to murmur. Being able to write, she spent many happy hours in exchanging letters with Christian friends, and in recommending her Saviour to those who knew Him not, but a stroke, which took away the use of her right hand, deprived her of this comfort. This great loss often caused her to weep, until one day, seeing on the wall a portrait of Milton after he was struck blind, she dried her tears, and thanked God she could yet read her Bible and see the glorious light of day.

Those that are able to move about, that live amongst, or frequently see the green fields, can form no adequate conception of the intense longing many have for such a privilege. Ann could well remember climbing the heath-clad hills, and looking on the wide spread landscape; she could tell of the time when she gathered the dasies, bluebells and buttercups; and often had a strong desire once again to have a glimpse of long lost scenes. Her room being small, and but one place for her bed, she could not look through the little window. One of her friends, hearing of her wish, fixed a lookingglass in such a position that, through the window, it reflected a green patch of rising ground behind the house. She shouted with delight, exclaiming " A green field! a green field! oh, how beautiful! how beautiful!"

In a letter received from her, written I think with the left hand, she says,—

"Language would fail to tell what Jesus has done for me, what kind Christian friends I have had, especially H. W. W., who has been to me a mother,—and what a faithful and affectionate nurse for all these years. Oh! I have proved the Lord true to His promise in every case. All may put their trust in Him, especially poor invalids, for He will never leave or forsake them that believe on Him."

No doubt the joys of this life are many to those that receive them with thankful hearts. The Christian in every state has great possessions here, but greater in prospect, and his faith, stretching over Jordan's streams, beholds fairer fields beyond the flood, and hopes to bask in happier climes. The blessedness of God's children, in sickness or in health, living or dying, none but God's children know.

Ann, like the poor man at the pool of Bethesda, has now been laid on her bed for thirty-eight years. That feeble, afflicted man had no friend to help him into the healing pool, until he met with Jesus, the feeling Friend of all. He then heard this short sentence, "Take up thy bed and walk," and in amazement he rose, not only able to walk but to carry his bed;—a lesson to all, that, when Christ bids us carry our burdens, He will give us strength to carry them. He found Christ at the end of his thirty-eight weary years, Ann found Him at the beginning; for at nineteen she enjoyed the sweet consciousness of sins forgiven. Christ could long since have raised her from her bed as He did the cripple at the pool side, for all power is His; but it is quite as great a miracle to give grace and patienoe to meekly and even joyfully suffer, as to take the cause of our suffering away. And, in this respect, the thirty-eight years bedridden Christian at Kendal, is as much a monument of God's goodness and power as the healed man of Bethesda; and no doubt as willing as he was to give all the glory to Him. And, from the little cottage in Strickland Gate, comes forth another witness that can stand side by side with Paul, and like him say, "There is laid up for me a crown." NAOMI,

We now leave the border towns of Westmoreland, and descend into one of the manufacturing districts of Lancashire, to visit another of my sick friends and one not the least interesting.

Those who have attempted to trace the course of the River Eoche, from the various little rills at its source to its junction with the IrwelL will have observed manybends and windings as it wends its way amongst rocks and woods, and well cultivated fields. In several places, the scenery on the banks 'presents great variety, and is often grand and imposing. Many cotton and woollen mills, for the purpose of obtaining water or steam power, have been built on the banks of the river, giving employment to some hundreds of the inhabitants.

At one of these mills, called Hooley Bridge, near Heywood, Naomi, the subject of this sketch, was at one time a healthy, cheerful, active labourer, and, like thousands of young people found in these mills, could sing the sweet hymns learned at the church and Sunday school, amidst the rumbling and rattle of machinery. She can sing yet, but under greatly altered circumstances. Her voice mingles not now with her fellow workers at the loom, or with the sublimer songs of the sanctuary, but in her lonely cottage chamber, upon a bed of pain.

Naomi was about sixteen years of age when a spinal weakness, felt by herself, became apparent to others. The means adopted to stay its progress being ineffectual, she gradually sank beneath its influence, until she became utterly unable longer to walk the short distance from her home to the mill; and in a few months her feebleness was so great, that she had not strength to rise from her chair. Ultimately she became so helpless that she was forced to remain continually in bed.

Sickness is sickness at any time of life. Even in old age, after having moved and mingled in the mazes anrl bustle of the ever-rolling current of active, busy scenes, it is sad to have the energies prostrated, the course of action arrested, and to be bound down in the corner with trembling limbs, able to move only at the will of others, or lie on the couch feeble and helpless, until the weary wheel of life stands still. Though this condition to the old may to some extent be looked for and expected, yet much patience and resignation is required to endure it. But to be smitten down in the very spring of life. when the world's pleasures are just dawning, and joyous hope daily brightening,—when the thorns and thistles of life, yet neither seen nor felt, are covered over with emerald leaves and scented flowers, then to fall from the ranks of healthy, cheerful, merry companions, with blighted prospects and dark forbodings, needs something more than earth can give to prevent madness or absolute despair.

Such was the condition of Naomi, ten years ago, and such it still remains. During the first three years of her helplessness, she had some relief from the weary hours, in being able to refresh her mind with the pleasures of reading. For this privilege she was very thankful, and greatly prized it; but, at the end of three years, intense pains in the head began to seriously affect her eyes. After a time, these pains were followed by dimness, darkness, and at last by utter blindness. Then The glorious sun, the moon, the stars, The hills, the dales, the fields, the flowers, on which Naomi had often looked with innocent delight, all disappeared in blackness and darkness. Yes, Naomi was Blind.

Was not the first burden laid on our greviously afflicted sister sufficient 1 Was it not enough to be for three years absolutely deprived of the power to raise herself from her bed, and all the time dependent on others for a crust of bread or a drop of water? Could not this deeper wound have been spared her 1 Surely the cross at first was heavy enough, but to be

"Shut out from the living whilst among the living;
Dark as the grave amidst the bustling world;
At once from business and from pleasure barr'd;
No more to view the beauty of the spring,
Nor see the face of kindred or of friend. "

Let Naomi herself answer these questions. The Bard of Avon draws well the horrors of blindness, but there are deeper depths of pleasure than worldly poets knowThe secrets of the Lord are with them that fear Him, and He will show them His covenant. And the nearer we get to God, the more we shall know His secrets, and better understand His covenant. He that tints the lily, clothes the grass, and notices the falling sparrow, numbers the hairs on the heads of His children. This Naomi firmly believes, for she is one of His children; she has the utmost confidence in. the declaration that "all things work together for good to them that love God;" and she knows that sickness, blindness, and de pendence are amongst the "all things." All the love of angels and of men falls infinitely short of the love of Naomi's Saviour. This she feels, and it is to her a real light, a heavenly radiance, shining into her happy soul.

On one of my visits to see Naomi, I was much concerned about her painful condition. She was unusually sore in body, and the pains in her head were more frequent. I thought it possible that, for a few pounds, a softer substance, placed under her weary frame, might considerably relieve her, and perhaps prevent the pains in her head; and through the kindness of those friends who trust me with money for the poor, I was able to purchase a water bed, which was to her au unspeakable boon.

It is now ten years since Naomi, through weakness and feebleness of body, became unable longer to attend the calls of the factory bell, or join those Sabbath gatherings that she so dearly loved in the school and church, of which she is a member. During seven of these years, the orbs of day have been closed, and she has been in one perpetual night. Milton's lines,—

"Dark, dark, dark, amidst the blaze of noon;
Irrecoverably dark, total eclipse;
Without all hope of day,

are powerfully descriptive of Naomi's condition, but her faith in the love of Christ sustains her, and she is another evidence that there is no condition of life that transcends the power of religion to relieve. Her resignation to God's will is amazing, and the sweet peace arising from Divine love flowing through her happy soul, wonderfully cheers her.

I now leave poor, afflicted, blind Naomi, quoting her words at our last interview,—" For I reckon that the suffering of this present life are not worthy to be compared with the glory that shall be revealed in us." ELIZABETH.

Let Us now call on Elizabeth, the last, but not the least, of our Sick Friends, residing at Bolton in Lancashire.

When Bolton had only one-half of its present inhabitants, when a few benevolent persons met to talk about the temporal circumstances of Samuel Crompton, before this generation appeared, and long before Bolton sent a member to parliament, or could boast of a mayor and corporation, the subject of this sketch was laid helpless on a sick-bed. In a group of cottages, called Union Buildings, now pulled down to make room for the railway, resided a labouring man of the name of Hill, with a wife and five children, of which Elizabeth was the eldest. Up to the age of sixteen, she did what she could to earn her own bread, and was a great help to her mother. Then weakness of the spine set in, and laid her utterly prostrate. She had been eighteen years in this condition when the house was pulled down, and, when removed, so entire was her paralysis, that she had to be carefully carried, as if in her coffin, on the shoulders of four men—the doctor walking by her side,—and quietly laid in the cottage she now occupies in Great Moor Street.

Those who have read "Priscilla," will remember that she often corresponded with Elizabeth. Fellow sufferers have kindred feelings, weeping with them that weep. It was through reading those letters that *I* first became acquainted with Elizabeth, and since then I have often had the privilege of sitting in her homely cottage, and hearing her tale of trials and triumphs. Speaking of her earlier years, she said,—

"When I first became convinced that there was little or no hope that I should ever recover, and sawthat I must be a burden and continual source of anxiety to my parents, I wished to die. Oh, how I besought the Lord then to take me, in mercy to others! My father's wages were sometimes very small; my little sisters and brothers were too young to earn anything; the direst poverty visited our home, and we were frequently reduced to the last morsel of bread. One Saturday, I felt quite faint for the want of food. There was nothing for any of us. My mother was greatly distressed, for she did not know what to do. I covered my face in bed, and wept and prayed that God would send us help, and, while I was weeping and praying, a man came in with a basin of broth and five shillings. This deliverance greatly affected my mother. She showed me the broth and the money, saying,— "How could the man know we were starving *V* "Mother," I replied, "the Lord sent him. " "When the man saw our condition, he went and told a good Christian lady

what he had seen. She came and told us she was just setting out for a month's pleasure to Blackpool, and was glad she had heard of our case before she had left. She informed us she had ordered a person to see us weekly until Bhe returned, when she would see to us herself. This lady was kind to me as long as she lived; she is dead now, and so are many of my old dear friends. But the Lord raises up new ones, and I wish, Mr. Ashworth, you would tell all God's afflicted children, that He who cares for the sparrows will not forget us."

No doubt many of Elizabeth's old friends are gone. Many ministers of the Gospel that have read and prayed at her bed-side—many benevolent Christians, young and old, that sought her house as a means of grace, have gone to their account; but others rise up, to whom she can tell her hopes and joys, and with whom she can join in songs of praise.

Having to attend a meeting in Bolton, I called in Moor Street, with a small present sent from my friend at Stratford. Elizabeth had that day been very happy, telling her dear, patient, loving, God-fearing sister, who has nursed and attended to her wants for many years, that some blessing was coming that day, but what it would be, she could not tell. On putting the little money I had brought into her hands, she looked at it, then at me. She was so surprised that her thin hands lost the power to hold it, and it fell on the bed.

"Sister!" she exclaimed, "sister! the blessing is come! I told you it would. Oh! sister, we will have a better fire now, and a little stronger tea. Oh, do help me to praise the Lord for His goodness, for He is better to me than He is to anybody in Bolton!"

Hear this, ye that fret, murmur, and pine, under little clouds and little trials; and ye that doubt, and weep, and fear lest God should forget to be gracious. Here is one of His children who, for Forty-two Years, has lain helpless on a sick-bed,—so helpless, that if that bed was on fire, she could not move; yet she is rejoicing and praising her dear Saviour for His goodness, and declaring that He is better to her, than to any of

her neighbours. And hear this, ye who tell us that the religion of the Bible is a cunningly devised fable. Ask Elizabeth and her answer will be,

"On this my steadfast soul relies,—
Father, Thy mercy never dies."

I have often felt my weakness, both in speaking and writing, but never more than in preparing these short sketches. What tongue or pen can give the biographies of lives both remarkable and monotonous *1* We have records of heroines, thrilling accounts of Boadicea, of the Maid of Orleans, of Grace Darling, Elizabeth Fry, Miss Nightingale, and others, all full of interest; but may not a nobility of soul be as much manifested in meekly bowing to a painful providence, as boldly performing the most glorious deeds?

I now take leave of my Sick Friends for the present; others still remain, of which something may yet be said. But I leave them with a conviction that, though they have unitedly been in pain, affliction, and helplessness for *one hundred and sixty-five years,* yet they are amongst the happiest creatures in this world. They may go down to their graves in silence, but they have taught a lesson to thousands; and that lesson is, that heaven's brightest beams can pierce the darkest cloud.

AMONGST the many callers at my house and office during the past year, there was one young man who, like most beggars, tried to look as sheepish as possible. Pulling off his hat, and looking to the ground, with a pitiable whine he said,—

"If you please, will you relieve me?"

"What is your trade, my young man?" I asked.

"A cabinet-maker, sir," was his answer, still whining.

"What age are you?" I again asked.

"Six-and-twenty, sir."

"Are you in good health?"

"Yes, sir; but I cannot get work,"—still whining.

I had been standing on the door-step, in my back yard, during this conversation, but, stepping down, I stood beside him, and, taking off my hat, said, "Now, my young man, look at me." Then, holding down my head, and trying to look as pitiable and sheepish as he did, I, in the same doleful whine, said,—

"If you please, will you relieve me *1* If you please, will you relieve me?" Then, looking him right in the face, I asked him what he thought of me. But he was too much astonished to speak. Then, putting on my hat, and requesting him to do the same, I said,—

"My young man, here you are, in good health and strength, with a good trade, and work plentiful, and you know it; yet you are sniffling and whining at people's doors, with your 'Please, will you relieve me *1* Why, man, if you had the spirit of a sparrow you would never so degrade yourself. Hold up your head, shake yourself, look into God's blue sky, and be a man. Here is sixpence; and now, let that be the last money you ever beg. Work, man, work, and no more whining. Whistle, and sing, and work, and be happy."

I thought for a moment he would have refused the sixpence. His face was red with indignation; and when he did take it he returned no thanks, but walked rather quickly away.

About four months after, the same young man called again, and, gently moving his hat, asked, with a smile, if I knew him.

"I do not, my young friend," I replied.

"Do you remember giving a young man, that came to your back door begging, a good blowing up, and mimicking him, whining, and saying, 'Please, will you relieve me *1*'"

"Yes, I think I do."

"Well, sir, I am that young man; and look, sir, I am now worth six pounds, all got by working, not whining and begging. I got employment the same day; and every hour that terrible whine, and 'Please, will you relieve me *1*' has been ringing in my ears. Oh! I could have shot you that day. But you did me a great kindness, for I did shake myself, and look into God's blue sky, and work. I have never been in a public-house since, for it was there I learned to be idle; and I am returning to my parents a new man. I wished first to call and tell you. And now, Mr. Ashworth, I beg

you will serve every young man as you served me, for it will be the best thing you can do for them. Good day, sir, and thank you for what you have done for me."

What a mercy for this young man, that the iron bands of indolence were snapped before they had for ever bound him in their fatal coils! A few months, or years, might have dragged him into the abyss of shame, infamy, and crime, inseparable from a life of idleness. For idleness is a self-inflicted curse; a sin against God and man; the parent of almost every evil. Its victims are legion. George, the principal subject of this narrative, was one of them; and I pray that this sketch of his life may be a warning to many.

George, in his early life, and after he was married, was by trade a hand-loom cotton weaver,—at one time a good business. He resided in the neighbourhood of Rochdale, where hand-loom weaving—both cotton and woollen—constituted the principal occupation of the inhabitants, and by which many of the careful and industrious have risen to great wealth. But George, like many weavers of this period, would only work three or four days a-week, however much "pieces" might be required by his employers; for the more labour was wanted, the less he cared about it. Like thousands of such characters, then as now, he had the greatest 'difficulty to tell what to do with the Sunday. The day God has given for special blessings hung the most heavily on his hands. Most of this precious day he spent in bed, until he became so tired that he got up to rest. Towards evening, if the night was too light for other purposes, he would get his pack of cards, and go out amongst his companions, drinking and cardplaying. This card-playing was to George what it has been to many—both rich and poor, high and low, vulgar and polished, old and young—a terrible besetment, bringing in its train untold evils; it is one of Satan's principal snares, and specially adapted to the indolent, thoughtless, and profligate.

There is an old Spanish proverb, "If Satan finds a man idle he sets him to

work." George was often found idle; for, besides lounging in bed the most of the Sunday, he seldom went to work on the Monday He would go miles to a foot-race, a dog-race, or a dogfight, where he was sure to meet with the most idle of the country; for like and like always go together. Towards Tuesday noon, or Wednesday morning, he began thinking about his loom; and his poor wife, besides doing her own weaving and housework, had very frequently to help him with his piece, by working during the night.

The wife of George was one of the most melancholy looking creatures I ever saw. She was tall, thin, with high cheek-bones, black hair, and had once been good looking. She was cleanly in her habits; and, I well remember, her principal dress consisted of a bedgown, then generally worn, a quilted green worsted petticoat, a white linen cap, with full screen, a crimson cloak, and black bonnet. She seldom entered any of the neighbours' houses, and seemed to avoid company, except when she attended a cottage service held in the neighbourhood on Sunday evenings. She always seemed sad; I never saw her smile, for her husband, besides being idle, was a great tyrant to her and the children, as most idle husbands are. But he was something more than either indolent or tyrannical; which, when she discovered it, made her miserable indeed. She had trouble enough before; but, when she found out what her husband really was, her sorrow was greatly increased.

Oh idleness! idleness! thou parent of many sins,— thou nurse of every crime,—thou Dead Sea, that swallowest up every good thing,—thou grave of every virtue, —what wretchedness hast thou produced! Thou art a most fruitful source of temptation; a field where the enemy sows many tares. The idle man's heart is Satan's workshop; he travels so slowly that poverty soon overtakes him. He will not plough, and he begs in harvest; he is always looking for something turning up, instead of working to turn up something.

It has been my lot to mingle much

with every description of self-inflicted misery,—in the prison, the union, the night-house, and penitentiary; in the streets. in dens of infamy, in homes of squalor, filth, and rags, and I believe that most of the appalling wretchedness I have witnessed springs from idleness, especially amongst the young men and young women. I am grieved to say—but a conviction of its truth, and a hope it may do good, compels me to declare—that a seven out of every ten of the fallen women prowling about our streets, are there because they are idle; they prefer a life of infamy to a life of honest industry. I have found homes of mercy for many such; but, finding they had to work, they soon left. I have obtained places of service for them amongst kind people, who engaged them with the intention of helping in their reformation, but very few hava remained; the places invariably being *too hard.* Tho injury inflicted by the curse of idleness, on either man or woman, can never be told.

The discovery made by George's wife, that so distressed her, took place late one dark evening. She had often been surprised that he never wanted to go out when it was moonlight; but, if the night was dark, he would frequently be absent till three or four in the morning. And she had noticed, with grief, that though their children were poorly clad, he never seemed to care for them, though he kept himself well-clothed,—how, she could not tell. She had once ventured to ask him how he got his new clothes; but he replied with such a terrible oath,—" What is that to you?" that she durst not ask him again.

The night we mention, George went out about ten o'clock. It was very dark and stormy. His wife asked him where he was going, and begged of him to stop at home; but he told her to mind her own business, and not meddle with his. The moment he was gone she burst into tears, and walked about the house almost wild with fear. She trembled from head to foot, and all desire for rest or sleep departed. Hour after hour she waited for his return, weeping, walking, sitting, kneeling, praying. For the poor thing sought help from Him who has

promised to help in the time of trouble; who never turns a deaf ear to the cry of the sorrowful; who sees every tear, and counts every sigh, and who mercifully invites the burdened and heavy-laden to come to Him for rest.

Hour after hour she waited. The candle died out, and the last embers of the flickering fire blackened in the grate; still she waited. She often started, thinking she heard his footstep. At last, certain of his approach, she hastened up stairs, fearing his anger if he found her below. She quickly undressed, and leant out of bed listening to hear his movements. He gently opened the door, went into the weaving room, and was there some time,—what doing, she could not tell. He then went to bed, without speaking one word, and it was near noon the following day before he rose to begin weaving.

A few days after, two constables, armed with a searchwarrant, came to seek for stolen goods. After a long search, they found several pieces of gold and silver plate hid under a flag. George had been house-breaking; the goods were owned, and he was sent to prison. When his time expired he returned home, but not to the home he had left; for his disgraced wife and children had removed from the village to hide their shame.

For several months after his liberation, George attended better to work, and the family began to improve in circumstances. His poor wife hoped the worst was past; but when dark evenings came again, he was more than once out the whole night, and the piece he ought to have woven in a week was in the loom for a month;—his idle habits had returned. One day the whole country was alarmed by the report that a dreadful robbery, with violence, had been committed at Hopwood Hall, near Middleton. Again George was apprehended, and some of the stolen property found in his possession.

At the time of this second robbery I was a young lad, and went to the free-school, in Kedcross-street, Koch, dale. James, the youngest son of George, was in the same class. One evening, he

asked me to go with him to the prison, in Rope Street, to enquire if they would let him see his father. He could not get admission, hut he put his mouth to the lock-hole, and called out,

"Father I Father I"

"Is that you, James *I*" replied his father. "If it be, tell your mother to come and see me to-morrow."

"Do you want her to bring you anything, Father *I* ' said the poor lad, weeping.

"No, nothing but my night-cap," was his father's answer.

James lived near to me, and we returned home together. He wished me to call with him, and tell his mother what his father wanted, saying,—

"I cannot tell her without orying, and she will cry too."

The mother went the following day to see her husband, and called at the school for James on her return. Her eyes were red with weeping. She feared to go the highway, shunning every one she knew, and we came through the fields, past the Oakenroad, Capterhood, and the Pitts, coming out at Passmonds. Just behind the farm-house at Pitts there is a brow; on the top of this brow James and his mother sat down, for she was greatly distressed. She had never spoken a word from calling at the school, but now her feelings overpowered her. She threw her arms round the neck of her sobbing child, and they both wept aloud. I stood a few yards from them, with tears running down my young cheeks. She sat there till it was dark, and when she arose she took hold of both our hands, and we walked out the narrow, dark road in silence. A few words she said, only a few, but I have never forgotten them:—

"My dear boys, never be idle, never steal; pray to God to make you honest and good. And you, James, do be a good lad, for your mother's sake."

We both promised, and promised, I am sure, very solemnly. James, I think, is now in heaven, and I hope the writer, through the mercy of a dear crucified Saviour, is on the way there.

George, with other two men,—John Taylor and Thomas Lang, charged with the same robbery, were eexamined before the magistrates, and all three sent, heavily ironed, to Lancaster castle, to await their trial at the next assizes.

How many idle men have entered through the arch of the frowning walls of Lancaster Castle;—entered, too, *because theywereidle!* for indolence wasat the foundation, at the very root of their crimes. How many idle men and women are, at this moment, pacing those narrow dens like wild beasts, or lying on their iron beds in sullen wrath, or writhing with remorse from the fiery stingings of a guilty conscience, or sinking in despair, or, where the soul is not yet callous, thinking of homes by them made desolate,—of relatives by them made to blush with shame,—of wife and children made by them to weep and sigh in hopeless sorrow! Oh, indolence! indolence!—thou proof and scourge of man's foul sins, what crimes have sprung from thee!

I well remember the intelligence reaching Rochdale that George was condemned to death; and I also remember that day poor James, his son, could not eat his dinner, but gave it away to the boys in the school. Poor lad! he was in great trouble. His distracted mother set out for Lancaster, to ask permission to have a last interview with her husband, and to beg his body. The sorrow-smitten creature travelled on foot many weary miles on her melancholy errand.

Oh I virtuous woman, thou wert made
Like heaven's own pure and lovely light,
To cheer life's dark and desert shade,
And guide man's erring footsteps right.

And when the last, sad scene is past,
"Pis woman weeps upon his bier;
Silent, yet long her sorrows last;
Unseen she sheds affection's tear t

Both her requests were granted, and the night before his execution she was admitted into his cell.

In those parting moments, when holding the hand and looking into the moistened eyes of some dear friend whom we fear we shall never see again, the heart is often filled with irrepressible sorrow. To stand by the death-bed of some loved one, to hear their last whispered farewell, and witness their last sigh, has often bowed down the stoutest hearts. To take the last look of the closing grave,—closing over the remains of those for whom our affections were stronger than life or death, has brought many to the border of madness. All this is sorrowful enough; but what must it be for a wife and a mother to tako the last look, and speak the last parting word to her husband going to be hanged!

I believe in broken hearts; I believe there may be anguish so deep, so profound, that all human aid is utterly useless. But I also believe that there is *one* Hand that can bind up broken hearts, and that Hand sustained the wife of George.

After the interview, she took shelter in a cottage house in the town for the night. She thought not of rest, but wandered about the room all night, unable to speak. Early in the morning of that dreadful 20th of April, she heard the sound of many feet hastening to the castle, to get a good place for seeing the deathstruggles of a fellow-being. Drunkards, racers, dogfighters, thieves, and robbers—the scum and dregs of society,—singing obscene songs, whistling, shouting, laughing, and swearing,—hundreds of the lowest and laziest characters gathered round the gallows. Only such could bear to look upon such a scene; for a man that can take pleasure in seeing another man hanged, is not unlikely to be hanged himself.

George was executed. After he was cut down, his body was handed over to his trembling, sobbing wife. She had a coffin ready, and hired a cart to carry his remains to Rochdale. When the crowd of idlers had dispersed, the coffin was lifted into the cart, and she began to retrace her steps the wearisome, dreary miles, she had come. For a long time she walked alone behind the cart—walked until she was faint and footsore. Yet, weary as she was, she refused to ride, thinking it disrespectful to the dead. But, her strength failing her, she reluctantly consented to be lifted into the cart. Before she reached her home the evening came on; and, in the black and dark night, sitting beside the coffin containing the body of her dead husband, she passed the house in which they had lived when he committed the first robbery,—the house and home of her children,—and, in the darkness, arrived at the narrow court in Town Meadows, from which George was taken to his grave.

On my last visit to Kendal, to speak on behalf of the Benevolent Society of that town, I called at Lancaster, at the request of a lady friend of mine, to give an address to the poor mothers she had brought together for that purpose. Her father, a magistrate, had kindly obtained permission for me to look through the Castle; and, after the address, in company with the lady, I went through the small door of the massive arch of that ancient fortress. The moment the door closed behind us, painful and gloomy thoughts, mingled with other feelings, came rushing into my soul. I was distressed to think that such a huge prison was necessary in any part of this world. Towering walls and battlements, firm as rocks; grated windows of gloomy cells; iron doors to deep, dark dungeons; bolts, bars, chains, and gallows,—all told how terrible sin is in its consequences, even in this life. For Christ's redeemed children, sinners saved by grace, don't come here. Ob, how forcibly these engines of punishment for crime, these penal caverns, these doleful, silent cells, proclaim the glorious truth of the divine Word: "Godliness is profitable for all things, having the promise of the life *that now is.*" Again and again, while walking through the various scenes of this castle of misery, did I feel thankful for the blessed influence of that religion which had saved, protected, and guided me; for, had it not been for this, I might have been long since found amongst the felons of my country. So, like Paul, my boasting shall be in Christ only.

By the kindness of the Governor of the Castle, I obtained a copy of the records of the assizes, as far as related to the trial and sentence of George; and not till then did I know that he had two companions in the perpetration of the robbery, which was, at that time, a crime punishable with death. The record is as follows:—

"George, John Taylor, and Thomas Lang, tried at Lancaster assizas, March, 1822. George sentenced to death, and executed, 20th of April, 1822; the other two were transported for life;—for a burglary at the house of Mrs. Gregg, Hopwood, near Eochdale, in October 1821."

I also requested the Governor to show me the cell where George was confined the night before his execution. I entered: the heavy door was bolted and barrred, and in darkness I sat down on the foot of the iron bed, with strange feelings,— feelings not easy to describe. I then went to the fatal door, or window, looking from the castle to the churchyard,—the opening where George stepped out, pinioned and bound, to look his last look on this world before he was launched into eternity.

As I stood and looked on this mournful part of the old Castle,—mournful because of its painful associations, — and knew that it was the spot where many, in a moment, and in the prime of life, had been violently sent from an erring to an unerring tribunal,—I thought, and still think, that, if their melancholy end could be traced to its true cause, it might be written on the grave of thousands besides George, p?c toas fttttnetr, IMPRISONED, AND HANGED, BECAUSE HE WAS TOO IDLE TO WORK.

"He that walkoth with wise men shall be wise, but the companion of fools shall be destroyed."—Pbovbrbs xiii. 20.

WHEN concluding the narrative of "George," I thought I would never again write on so painful a subject; but a request from poor James Burrows, made only sixteen hours before his execution, that I would "make his mournful condition a warning to all young men," leaves me no choice in the matter; for how could I refuse him anything in that dreadful hour % I felt I could not, and promised to carry out his wish to the best of my ability.

I am no believer in dreams; neither do I despise them. No doubt they are often the result of certain physical conditions,—the tangled fragments of mental emotion, or the reflex action of our waking hours. It is probable that from this last cause I was greatly troubled in my sleep on the night of August 23rd, 1866, for I had been hoping, during the whole day, that the Home Secretary might possibly grant a reprieve to James,—prolong one life, and save Manchester from the demoralizing effects of a public execution. So deep had been the impression during the night, and so great was my anxiety about the young man, from knowing something of his family before they left Barnford, that in the morning I felt a strong desire to gain admission to his cell. I knew the difficulties would be great, for the condemned are very properly guarded from unnecessary intrusion.

On approaching the prison, I found crowds of people lounging about, and workmen engaged in fixing strong barriers across the streets. I entered, and requested one of the warders to forward my card to Mr. Thomas Wright. That venerable philanthropist soon made his Appearance, accompanied by Mr. Bagshawe, the patient, kind-hearted chaplain of the gaol. They both expressed their joy that I had come, and sent a joint request to the High Sheriff, Sir E. Armitage, for his permission to admit me to see the condemned prisoner.

And here I would mention a few incidents that transpired during the short time I was waiting for the order.

Outside the iron gates, and pressing against the bars, hundreds of very young, ragged, dirty boys and girls, were gathered, all of whom ought to have been at work or at school. Such a miserable and pitiable sight I never before beheld; nor could I help thinking that many in that youthful gathering were candidates for the prison, if not for the gallows, but not from any fault of their own. Poor things! doubtless many of them were the children of drunken or thoughtless parents.

Whilst looking on this mass of

squalid wretchedness, the police began to beat them back to make room for a procession of publicans, who were coming down the steps from the Brewster Sessions, that had just been held in the court-room. Here was a junction indeed —the victims and their destroyers. And these crimemanufacturers had been asking an extension of power to carry on their terribly ruinous business I Before they went out of the gates, they were in the right place; and all Brewster Sessions ought to be held in the New Bailey. If they were, and the wives and children of drunkards had the power of the keys, they would not soon be let out.

The High Sheriff having granted the urgent request of Mr. Bagshawe and Mr. Wright, we all three threaded our way through the gloomy, winding passages, past the grated window and bolted door of many a cell, until we reached the one occupied by James Burrows. Poor lad! he sat on a square buffet, reading a pictorial copy of Watts's "Divine Songs." The moment we entered he rose, and seemed glad at the return of his two venerable friends.

And here let me describe this unfortunate young man, not yet nineteen years of age. In height he was about five feet ten inches, and stout in proportion. He had glossy black hair, a full face, ruddy cheeks, and fair skin. He was clothed in the felon's dress,—a round jacket, and vest of party-colours (like patchwork), coarse woollen trousers, and a narrow black stock round his neck,— yet he looked a handsome, healthy, strong young man. As I gazed at him, and thought that, before noon the following day, his fine frame would he laid in a murderer's grave, I felt what language could never express.

On being introduced to him he took hold of my hand, and for some time held it in silence. But seeing the tears streaming down my face, he heaved a deep sigh and quietly sat down, burying his face in his hands. We all followed his example; and for a considerable time none of us could speak one word. James again sighed, and, laying his hand on my knee, said,—

"Do you remember, one Sunday,

speaking to rue and some other young men, who were pigeon-flying, near Thornam Lane, and telling us that Sabbath-breaking, dog-running, and pigeon-flying must come to a bad end?" "I think I do; for I have often spoken to young men, on the road from Rochdale to Middleton, about bad company, pigeon-flying, and Sabbath-breaking," I replied.

"Yes, you did; but we only laughed at you when you were gone, for we were a bad lot. Like and like go together; and wicked company has brought me to this. Living at an ale-house, going to ale-houses, and bad company have done it all; and it will do it for more beside me. Oh! I wish I had taken warning in time."

James again sighed, and, taking the book he had been reading from a small table, he opened it at the nineteenth page. Handing it to me, he folded his hands, and with a trembling voice began:— ' Almighty God, Thy piercing eye Strikes through the shades of night, And our most secret actions lie All open to Thy sight.

"There's not a sin that we commit Nor wicked word we say, But in Thy dreadful book 'tis writ, Against the judgment-day.

"And must the crimes that I have done Be read and published there *l* Be all exposed before the sun, While men and angels hear? Lord, at Thy foot ashamed I lie Upward I dare not look; Pardon my sins before I die, And blot them from Thy book." During the repeating of this hymn, James remained seated on the square buffet; but so intense had bis feelings become, that he now rose and fixed his eyes on the ceiling,—his hands still being clasped, and, with a bursting heart cried out, in the words of David, recorded in the fifty-first Psalm,—" Have mercy upon me, O God, according to Thy loving-kindness: according unto the multitude of Thy tender mercies blot out my transgressions. Wash me throughly from mine iniquity, and cleanse me from my sin. For I acknowledge my transgressions: and my sin is ever before me.

Create in me a clean heart, O God; and renew a right spirit within me. Cast me not away from Thy presence; and take not Thy Holy Spirit from me." He repeated the entire psalm, laying great emphasis on the 14th verse: —"Deliver me from *blood-guiltiness,* O God, Thou God of my salvation: and my tongue shall sing aloud of Thy righteousnesa"

While he was repeating the hymn and psalm, and especially the concluding words, James's voice seemed to be choking with intense agony. He let his hands fall, and, quietly sitting down, with quivering lip said,—" Christ Jesus came into the world to save sinners. Yes, He did. And what could I do without Him?" Then again springing to his feet, at the top of his voice he cried out, "Him that cometh to me, I will in nowise cast out;" and, turning quickly round to Mr. Bagshawe, he said, "That is the passage for me,—for poor James f O, when I first heard that passage, I grab'd it!—hope came when I first heard that, and I grab'd it!"

On expressing my surprise at his quoting the Scriptures so correctly, and informing him that I had understood from the newspapers that he could neither read nor write, he replied,—

"When I came here I knew nothing but wickedness. I did once go to the Sunday school in Bamford, before we removed from there to yon cursed alehouse; and I also went, a short time after we removed, to Thornam School. But I left, and joined bad and idle company, and soon lost all I had learned. Those schools look nice to me now!

"Lord how delightful 'tis to see, A whole assembly worship Thee, At once they sing, at once they pray, They hear of heaven, and learn the way.

"Yes, they learn the way, and if I had remained at the Sunday school, I should have learned the way too. That is a nice line; They learn the way.'" Then, looking at Mr. Bagshawe and Mr. Wright, he said,—

"These two dear friends have taught me all I know that is good; for I knew nothing but wickedness before I came here. I was a wandering sheep. I have

learned to read, and to write a little, and to think of my precious soul, since that dreadful day, thirteen weeks last Monday. Had I had a thousandth part of the religion outside these walls, that I have learned inside, I should have kept away from wicked companions, and never have come here. But like and like go together, and, Mr. Ash worth, tell all young men from me, four things:— 1. *To keep the Sabbath-day holy; 2. To go to some place of worship;* 3. *To keep from the alehouse;* and 4. *To keep out of bad and idle company.*

If they do these, they will never be imprisoned, transported, or hanged."

"What do you mean by thirteen weeks last Monday, James?" I asked.

"Mean! I think I mean enough," he replied. "It was the day poor John Brennan was murdered! 1 wonder God did not strike me dead that day, and send me to hell; and I do thank Him that He did not."

"And how could you do such a deed, James? For I hear you have confessed you did it"

"Do it! I wonder now how I could do it. When a man once begins to serve Satan, he does not know what he will make him do. But I have been led on by bad companions, and by one more wicked than the rest, who was always bragging of what he had done. I thought I would be as clever as him. I had nothing against Brennan, poor man, but I would have his money. After I had done the deed, the man that has been a curse to me had seven shillings and sixpence of the money,— five shillings of which went to pay off an ale-score he owed."

Here James's feelings so overpowered him that he rose, exclaiming,—

"What will become of John Brennan's poor wife and children! If I had any money, I would leave it all to them. Mr. Ash worth, can you get them something %"

I promised I would send what I could, and this seemed to give him some little comfort.

Let it not be supposed that I am one of those who can weep for the criminal, and forget the victim of his crimes; or wring my hands over the felon, and forget his foul deeds. Murder is murder, whether it be *one* that makes the villain, or *thousands* that make the hero. I hope mankind will ever look on the man of blood with horror. James Burrows was a great sinner, but he had been greatly sinned against. I shall not say one word about his parents or his family; James requested that I would not, and they have had trouble enough. But character is often transmitted from parents to children, and this fact ought to be more generally recognized than it is. There is as much difference in the natural dispositions of men, as in the breed of horses or dogs; and while the propensity to do evil is in all, some *inherit* it more than others. Surrounding circumstances, too, often favour, and even force its strong development, as in the case of James Burrows. Surely some sympathy may be shown for such, and some pity be legitimately bestowed on them. The sons and daughters of truly religious parents little know how much they have to be thankful for, enoiroled from childhood, as they have been, with good example, tenderness, love, and favourable influences. They are sheltered from those fierce temptations that might have been their utter destruction, body and soul. For nothing but Divine grace can restrain some characters; and the old Lancashire minister and martyr, John Bradford, was right, when, seeing evil-doers on the way to execution, he exclaimed, "But for the grace of God, there goes John Bradford!"—and many more may say the same.

Some have said, "Swing the wretch off, and have done with him, for he richly deserves it!" Few, very few, have had what they deserve; and I think that no man who knows his own heart would ever utter each unfeeling words., No; the good man mourns over these dreadful evidences of fallen humanity; but his very sorrow purifies his soul, and nerves him for greater good. The field of labour widens before him, and he sees he must still work on. Yes, brothers and sisters in the Lord's vineyard, work on! No one can tell how many scaffolds you have prevented being erected. Of one thing you may rest well assured, that you can never labour in vain In The Lord.

Just when I had promised James that the widow and children of his victim, should not be forgotten, whether from the sound of a bell, or some other cause, he knew it was four o'clock; and, with a deep sigh, said,—

"Sixteen hours; sixteen hours, and then!"

James knew that he could not live more than sixteen hours, for he neither expected nor wished for a reprieve. He frequently said he ought to die for his great crime, and he had a fear of again falling into bad company, either in prison or out, and his mind was entirely fixed on things eternal. Humanly speaking, he had sixteen hours to live; but how uncertain is human life! A young man, talking about the execution to one of his fellow-workmen, said,—"I will work overtime to-day, for I am going to see Burrows hanged on Saturday." But in six hours the young man's dead body lay waiting the coroner's inquest! Immediately after he had spoken the words, he fell from the top of a building in Bamford, and was killed on the spot. He went to his account before the man he was going to see executed! So uncertain is human life; and no man is wise who is not prepared for this uncertainty.

Seeing I was about to leave, James looked me in the face. I understood that look, and said,—"Yes, James, I will pray with you." James now loved prayer, and had prayed with his father, mother, and sister when they visited him in prison. We all four knelt down,— James first. He knelt at the small side table, his elbows resting upon it, with his hands clasped, and his face lifted towards the top of the cell. For a short time we knelt in silence; for my utterance was choked, and I felt that silence was more eloquent than words. I had prayed, in my feeble way, under many varied circumstances, with almost every variety of character, but never with a fellow-sinner within sixteen hours of his execution. Oh, how weak were words at that moment, and how my heart yearned for power to plead with the Friend of sinners on behalf of the poor doomed one that knelt sobbing by my side!

After prayer, we all rose up except James, who still remained with clasped and uplifted hands and closed eyes, repeating his favourite promise,—"Him that Cometh unto me I will in no wise cast out;" and, in the anguish of his spirit, he cried out,—" Yes, Lord, I come! Jesus, I come! O, I come, I come!

"Just as I am—without one plea,
But that Thy blood was shed for me,
And that Thou bidst me come to Thee,
0 Lamb of God, I come.
"Just as I am—and waiting not
To rid my soul of one dark blot;
To Thee, whose blood can cleanse each spot,
0 Lamb of God, I come.
"Just as I am, though tossed about,
With many a conflict, many a doubt,
Fightings within, and fears without,
O Lamb of God, I come."

With a power and an earnestness I never before witnessed, he repeated the whole of that beautiful, brokenhearted sinner's hymn, before he rose from his knees! I need not say how affecting was the scene.

Another favourite hymn he constantly repeated was,

"Nearer, my God, to Thee, nearer to Thee." Referring to it he remarked to the chaplain, "Sir, if I were as near to God now, as I was far from Him when I came into this prison, I am very near Him at this moment."

On taking my leave, he again requested me to speak to young men, and warn them of bad company and Sabbath-breaking. He also desired to make me some present, and looking round the cell, he took from the small table the pictorial copy of Watts's Hymns he was reading when we entered, turning down the leaf at the lines, "Almighty God, Thy piercing eye." The Chaplain, Mr. Bagshawe, at our joint request, wrote the inscription, and Mr. Wright witnessed it. The words are, *Presented to Mr. fahn Jlshworth, of0lochdaZe, in the cell of the Jfew sBailey, Salford, iy fames burrows, on the 24-th of August. 1866, the day-before his execution. Signed*

I now took leave of the doomed

young man, but could not, during the whole night, forget the sad interview, and in the morning, at the moment I believed he would be ascending the scaffold, we read at family prayer his favourite 51st Psalm, and knelt down, not forgetting poor James.

Mr. Bagshawe, the Chaplain, kindly sent me the following particulars of his last hours.

"You saw him the afternoon of the last entire day he lived; I left him about eleven in the evening, returning about six in the morning. He was glad to see me, and we at once began to talk about what was the nearest his heart,—those divine and living truths that live and abide for ever. We then knelt down before that God, at whose bar James would in two hours appear. He was very calm and humble; not a word or action unbecoming. He said,—

'"I could shed tears day and night, but that would not save me; Christ only can save. I have heard about persons dying game, but I hope to do nothing foolish. It is not what man may think, but what God thinks that concerns me now.'

"The strange, sickening sounds, arising from the surging thousands outside the prison walls, we heard very plainly, and the noise was truly dreadful. I feared its effect on James, but it did not move him. Seven o'clock struck, and he again fervently prayed in the words of the 51st Psalm, and all knelt down, Mr. Wright engaging in prayer.

"At twenty minutes to eight, the High Sheriff, Under Sheriff, the Mayor of Salford, the Governor of the prison, and the hangman, came into the cell. The Under Sheriff asked James if he had any communication to make. At his request I produced a paper he had signed, acknowledging his guilt, and read it aloud. He then repeated the Confession, and the Collect for the 21st Sunday after Trinity, with such earnestness, that many, and even Calcraft, the hangman, shed tears. After he was bound the procession moved, and I read the service,— 'I am the resurrection and the life,' &c.

"Through the long dark cell-yard, and up to the foot of the gallows, Burrows seemed absorbed in praying, without an omission, the whole of the 51st Psalm. The procession paused, and he emphatically uttered the Lord's prayer, once more, and the entire hymn,—"Just as I am," with much energy. I then closed the service, and, my work being done, took leave of him. Ere I reached my room I heard the heavy thud of the falling floor of the scaffold, and all was soon over."

I thank Mr. Bagshawe for this account of the last moments of poor James, and, like him, I would draw a veil over the scene on the scaffold;— that scene which twenty thousand upturned faces beheld, but which I have no wish to describe.

A coffin had been provided, and a grave was in readiness, and, in a few hours, the body of the victim of bad companions was buried in that grave. As I stood beside it, I remembered standing over the graves of those who had been executed at Newgate, London, and on the mounds under the willows, in Kirkdale, Liverpool. Now I stood on the One, the first, and, I hope, the last in this melancholy spot, and as I stood, I again felt how terribly true are the words of the Holy Book. Thousands of young men and young women, who, by sin in its various forms, are cut down in the midst of their years, or left to linger out a life of suffering and sorrow, worse than death, could, with a voice loud as the roar of the raging storm, bear their testimony to the truth of these words: "he That Walketh With Wise Men SHALL BE WISE, BUT THE COMPANION OP POOLS SHALL BE DESTROYED." THERE is something very impressive, and, if seen aright, profitable and instructive, in marking time's silent power. Ancient nations and ancient cities,— halls and palaces of ancient song, moulder into ruin, and are numbered with the things that were. The old tree, and the old house, sacred from many endearing associations, crumble into dust, and succeeding ages know them only by tradition. But nowhere is the touch of time's fatal finger seen and felt so distinctly as in the gaps made amongst our relations and friends, or in the changes in our schools and congregations; —

here his doings are often painfully visible, and annual records have to tell of their death. The "Chapel for the Destitute" shares largely in these changes, for, in proportion to our numbers, we have many aged and infirm people; and this year two of these ancient ones, amongst others, have fallen from our ranks—old John, and old Mary his wife. One is dead, and the other is dying; and two more primitive creatures it would, perhaps, be difficult to find.

Old John was small in stature, had thin grey hair, carried his head on one side, walked with a short, quick step, and leant heavily on a stout hazel stick. Mary, like her husband, was short in stature, had grey locks, was very thin in flesh, and had a sharp nose. She wore a well-washed printed dress of very ancient pattern, but no crinoline, a scuttle-shaped bonnet, a white linen cap, with a large border round her small face. In their later days they were so infirm that they had to depend on friends to help them up the steps of the Chapel; and, when they made their appearance, persons sitting in the aisles rose to make way for the feeble couple to reach their accustomed place amongst the aged worshippers near the platform.

John, in his younger days, had been a very hardworking man. For more than thirty years he had been a "slubber" in a woollen mill, and during the whole of that time he had never once entered a place of worship, except at a funeral. Like thousands, John, during these thirty years, lived very much like a donkey—eating, working, sleeping, drinking; only the donkey never drank until it tumbled into the gutter, which John often did. But he adopted one plan which drunkards might imitate with advantage,—he got drunk at the public house which was nearest his own home; for he said drink was so bad to carry, that he did not like to carry it far. His little wife had not only a sharp nose, but a sharp tongue; and the sound of that tongue, at the door of the drinking-house, was a signal for John to finish his cup. Some wives fetch their drinking husbands home when they want to taste a little themselves; but Mary would never touch a drop, nor would she prop him up by taking hold of hia arm when going home, for she said people could not tell which was the tipsy one. If he fell, he fell, and

A she would give him a long or short lecture until he could gather up his legs and walk. Her speeches on these occasions did not vary much. When he tumbled she would say,—

"There—down again, down again! Thou should bring the publican with thee to help thee up; thou hast bought his fine wife another yard of ribbon for her fine cap, and when thou buys her another yard thou wilt roll in the mud again. I wonder what I was doing when I wed thee; I wish it was to do again. Get up, this minute; get up!"

John took his wife's scolding very patiently; he would scramble to his feet, balance himself, and make another trial. He thought as well of his little wife as such characters generally do, and that is not saying much. For a man to pretend to love his wife, when he leaves her fretting, sorrowing, lonely, and often weeping because he is degrading and disgracing both her and himself, and spending the money that she needs for the requirements of the house,—for such a man to pretend to love his wife or children is downright hypocrisy: a man is what he *does*, not what he *says*. But there was one good thing about John— he never neglected his work for drink. He. would toil hard, at his toiling business, during the week, and have a short fuddle on the Saturday evening, and a longer one on the Sunday. His careful, plodding wife did the best she could; shekept their cottage clean, had a. tidy fire-side, a wellpolished set of mahogany drawers, and the stockings well-mended.

But what a life was this for two immortal beings, made in God's image, made capable of the highest enjoyments—sleeping, eating, working, merely dragging on an existence, and nothing more!—utter strangers to those higher and sublimer thoughts arising from intellectual aspirations; or those still grander and more enduring spiritual emotions springing from union and communion with the Fountain of purity and bliss. They lived as many live,— with no joyful greetings for the return of the blessed Sabbath morn; no longing for the sweet period mercifully given for the gathering of the sons and daughters of toil to those earthly sanctuaries emblematic of heavenly mansions. The cheerful intermingling of the followers of the Lamb, as they gathered from hill and dell round their various altars on the Lord's day, never found John or Mary joining in their happy assemblies. No; nor did they in their cottage home even kneel together in prayer, or open the pages of the Book of Life. They lived without God and without hope, consequently without joy and without peace; for let the world say what it willSolid joys and lasting pleasures None but Christians ever know.

Mary, in after-life, when speaking of this long, miserable, blank period, often said,—

"We lived like pigs, and worse than pigs, though we were thought to be as good as our neighbours. Many of them died in ignorance and sin, and I can never tell how it was that God spared our John and me; but there was not the same chance of knowing things then that there is now, and I think the poor were less cared for. There were not so many churches, schools, and chapels. There was one place of worship about two miles from where we lived, but the parson never went to see after any of us, except when we had a child christened; for we always brewed a peck of malt at a christening, and invited the parson to come; yet he was a very decent man, taking him altogether, for I never heard tell of him being drunk, though he liked a drop; but I think teetotal parsons are safest, for then they can say,—' Do as I do,' and folks will take more notice of what they say."

Mary's opinion may or may not be endorsed by all, but in one thing she was right,—churches, chapels, and schools have greatly multiplied, and the privileges of this day are immeasurably beyond what they were fifty years since. Old people then were ignorant of the simplest principles of Christianity, and often showed their Ignorance to an amazing degree. I know something of the old minister to whom Mary referred, and have often been to the church or chapel where he officiated for many years. One hot summer morning, as this minister was quietly wending his way up the rising ground leading to the church, in company with an old man, looking at the hard, cracked ground, and the brown, parched fields, he said to his aged friend,— "James, we must have prayers for rain to-day." James stood still, looked up at the sky, then at the waving branches of the trees, and quietly replied,—

"It won't do, minister; it will be of no use. You might a3 well whistle while the wind is where it is."

Foolish as was the reply, and strange as such ignorance may seem to us now, let us remember it is through our schools, and especially our Sunday schools, that we have been led to think differently; for now almost every child taught there could tell that old man that He who created the winds holds those winds in His hands, and both winds and clouds obey Him. We live in a glorious day, and we have glorious privileges, at least in this country. He that is a fool now, in things sacred and divine, is a fool because he will be a fool; but let him know, that to whom much is given, of him will much be required.

My first acquaintance with old John and Mary arose from seeing them at the chapel. Many have heard Mary tell of the first time she came. When repeating the story she would say:—

"I was wandering about in the streets one Sunday evening, and seeing a card at the door inviting all poor people that attended no other place of worship, I stood still and read it, saying to myself,—Chapel for the Destitute! Chapel for the Destitute! this is a new shop, and I think it is the shop for me, for I am destitute enough in all conscience, and I will see if they will let mo in. I went in and saw scores as poor as myself, and when they rose up and all began to sing, I began to cry. I never was so affected in my life. The hymn was,

'Come, let us join our cheerful

Bongs,
With angels round the throne.'

"After singing, the minister began to read out of the Bible the thirteenth chapter of Luke. I shall never forget that chapter. When he was reading that part which said, 'Except ye repent ye shall all likewise perish,' I thought, well I have done some things which I had better not have done, but I am not as bad as some that are here by a long way. But when he came to that part which says, Strive to enter in at the strait gate,' he stopped, and, looking at us all he said, 'How many present are doing what Christ here commands, striving *I* There is a time when we may enter the way to heaven, and a time when we cannot; when the door is shut we may strive, but then we shall strive in vain.' I felt very strange while he was reading and speaking. I am not striving, I thought, nor is our John, and if heaven's door is shut on us it will be a very sad thing.

"Before I came out of that place that night, I began to think I was as bad as anybody in it. I went home and told our John all about the chapel and what I had heard, and I said to him, I can understand yon man every word he says; he neither talks about Jews nor Gentiles, but about Jesus Christ coming to seek and save lost sinners; that we are all sinners, and that Christ died to save us all, and that, except we repent and receive this salvation, the door will be shut, and we shall perish.

"I was in good earnest while I was telling our John, and was vexed to see that he did not seem to care; but I said, 'If I live until next Sunday I shall go to yon place again, and thou shalt go with me.'"

Mary did not succeed ia persuading John to come the following Sunday, nor the Sunday following that; but she talked so much about the chapel, telling her husband all she could remember about the reading and sermons, and trying to induce him by kind words to make a promise to go with her, that at last he consented. She was so much afraid he would break his promise, that she got Matthew Shepherd, an old man in the neighbourhood, to call a little be-

fore the service time and encourage her husband to go. Between them they succeeded, and all three set out together. Mary took good care that her partner got as near to the preacher as possible, on account of his slight deafness, and two more attentive hearers could not be found in our congregation that evening.

As they were returning home after the service, Mary asked John how he had liked it, and if it was not true that they had been living like pigs.

"Well, I do not think I shall go again," replied John.

"Why *I*" asked his wife, in great alarm.

"Well, I don't like to be made uneasy, and I have felt very much so to-night; if what we heard be true, I have been wrong a long time."

"It *is* true, John, and we have both been living as if we had no souls, and it is quite time we began to cry for mercy, if it be not too late; and I do hope God will pardon us both, for I feel I cannot do as I am."

I was glad when I heard of the conversation of the old couple, but was still more pleased when I was informed that they had begun to pray together in their humble cellar, and to ask others to pray with them. The Spirit of God had wounded their consciences and troubled their souls, and is it not a mercy when sinners, high or low, rich or poor, are troubled on account of their sins *t* It is a fearful thing when a man is so hardened in his crimes that he is past feeling. One of the kings of France, Louis XIV. , said to Fenelon, "When I hear some men preach I am pleased, and with others I am edified, but when I hear you I am miserable and unhappy, and feel my sins." "Thank God for that," said Fenelon, "for if there be no feeling of need, there will be no crying for help." Fenelon was right. "God be merciful to me a sinner!" is, and ever will be, the stereotyped cry of every contrite spirit, and that cry from a breaking heart ever was and ever will be heard.

At the request of John and Mary, a part of our company of the "Destitute" went weekly to hold a prayer meeting in their cellar in Falinge-road; and glad the

old people were to receive them, for one of the true signs of either penitence or pardon is a love of prayer, —not simply praying, but loving to pray. I well remember attending one of these devotional gatherings. The company that day consisted of John and Mary, Matthew Shepherd, John Hamer, an old blind man, a street sweeper we called Ben, a half-wit called Eobert, and several others.

This Robert, or, as he is more frequently called,

Bobby, is a well known imbecile, about forty years of age. He has small, deep-sunk eyes, near to each other, a low forehead, a strange, vacant look, and is very harm i less. He regularly attends some place of worship, knows nothing about texts, but can always tell when it is twelve o'clock. He seems to hearken to all that is said, but if the preacher goes beyond the time, Bobby leaves him, and quietly walks out of the chapel. There is not one spark of intelligence in his countenance, but he can be moved to joy by a Sunday school procession, a tea party, or the singing of children; and if the preacher should mention Canaan, happy land, realms of the blest, glory, heaven, or Jesus, then he clasps his hands, smiles, and looks up, and seems truly happy; and he was happy that night.

I have been in many prayer meetings, and heard many strains of humble and exalted eloquence, but none more memorable than that evening in that cellar, amongst those simple-hearted worshippers. Old John prayed first, saying, after ho had repeated the Lord's prayer.

"O Lord, I thank Thee for Thy goodness to me and our Mary. We had nearly been lost, and should have been, but Christ Jesus saved us. What a mercy! how good Thou art, O Lord. Help us all to be good, and to praise Thee. Amen."

Mary, very modestly and tremblingly, prayed' after her husband, saying,

"Lord, Thou knowest what I want better than I can tell Thee, for I feel afraid to pray when so many are here. I can pray the best when our John and me are with our two selves; but Thou knows I can just say what Peter said,

Thou knows all things, Thou knows I love Thee. And I wish I could love Thee more, for Thou hast done wonderful things for all of us, and me especially, for once I was blind but now I see. Amen."

After singing a verse, we again all kneeled down, and old Matthew, always simple and earnest in prayer, said,

"O Lord, help me, and help to pray. I have had hard work to get down on my knees, for old age is making my joints very stiff. I know what that passage of Thy word means now, better than ever I did before, —the spirit is willing, but the flesh is weak. I find I am getting very weak but I love Thee, Lord, this very minute as much as ever I did in my life, and I think more; and if these old limbs are soon to tumble into the grave, well, it is all right, for I can truly say that if my heart and flesh faileth, Thou art the strength of my heart and my portion for ever. But I have one request to make, Lord; and oh! I do wish Thou would grant it before I die. Yon wicked son of mine, I think he gets more wicked every day; I am sometimes ready to wish he was either mended or ended. O that I could but see him converted, then I think I could die any minute. I would then say, with old Simeon,—now lettest Thou Thy servant depart in peace. And now, Lord, look at us all at Thy feet in mercy; Thou hast done great things for old John and Mary, for which I believe they are glad; and they may well be glad, for they have had a narrow escape; the door had been near shut. And, Lord, bless old blind John Hamer; I think sometimes thou hast perhaps made him blind to save his soul, for he thinks more about his soul now than he did when he could see. David said, before he was afflicted he went astray, and so have scores done besides David. Lord, bless us all, and make us what thou would have us to be at any price, for it will be the best for us in the end, and the end will soon come, and then I hope we shall all meet in heaven. Amen."

While old Matthew was praying, Ben, the street sweeper, a fine, healthy, middle-aged man, was much affected,

and, with a tremulous voice, said in his prayer,

"O, Lord, when I see these poor old creatures, and think I may very likely live to be as old as they are, I wonder whether I shall have grace to keep me faithful and patient, for I am sure I shall need it then. Well, the promise is, that as our day is so shall our strength be, and that will do both for me and them. Help us all to have our lamps trimmed; for to know they are trimmed it will make us happy, whether the Bridegroom comes soon or late. Amen."

It was well for Benjamin that his lamp was trimmed, for, in fourteen days after he offered that prayer, he was laid in his grave, though the most likely for a long life of any present at that meeting.

I repeat the simple prayers of these illiterate people, to show how their hearts were imbued with the love of God. The intelligent, educated Christian, when bowing before his Maker in the social means of grace, will necessarily clothe his thoughts and desires in more elegant language, but it does not follow that he gets nearer to the throne of grace. Simplicity in prayer is taught us by Him who is the medium of all effectual prayer; and if the prayers of these simple people appear in the eyes of some to be irreverent, my experience amongst many such has convinced me that this is more in appearance than in truth.

In these cellar prayer meetings, a scene both painful and pleasing was often witnessed. Feeble and infirm as old John was, he would kneel down during the devotion. No persuasion could induce him to remain standing or seated; for he had a strong conviction that in prayer he ought to bow down both soul and body. But after prayer he had always to be assisted to rise. His wife, the moment she rose, would walk across the floor, take hold of his arm, and help him to his feet In their younger years she could scold him, and refuse him the helping hand, when he lay drunk in the ditch; but now, with tears of thankfulness, she supports his trembling limbs,—raising him up, and placing him in his chair.

Great care was taken that John and

Mary should not be without food, clothing, or attendance. They had a small allowance from the parish-funds, and many kind friends added to their comforts by daily seeing to their requirements.

But the time was now come when their increased infirmities made it impossible for them longer to attend their "blessed chapel," as they called it. Old Matthew and others had brought them there, and taken them back as long as they could. On my last visit, Mary expressed a conviction that her time was short, and spoke with remarkable calmness of her approaching end.

'Her only concern was about leaving her old partner behind, and she frequently desired that, if it was God's will, they might be both buried on the same day. But this desire was not granted, for on the morning of the 27th of February, 1866, in the seventy-seventh year of her age, her last lingering whisper died on her tongue, and that last whisper was—" Mercy's free."

Mary now lies buried in the free ground of the Rochdale Cemetery, and John's days are fast drawing to a close. His mind often wanders, and then he forgets that his aged partner is gone. He asks her to sing for him; he talks to her about the chapel, and wonders how soon old Matthew will call for him;—tells her if no one calls for him he will try to go himself, and. wants to know how it is she never speaks to him now. Because she does not answer he weeps, and begs her to speak to him just once more. Much of his time is spent in sleep, but during his conscious hours his mind is evidently fixed on eternal things. He prays for the people at the "Destitute," prays for all those who go to visit the sick and poor, and prays that he may soon be taken to heaven. Soon that prayer will be heard; and I believe that, when the pages are read in the Lamb's Book of Life, on these pages will be found the names of John And Mary. AGES to come will hear with sadness and sorrow of the mournful catastrophe, involving the instant destruction of over three hundred men and boys, at Barnsley, in Yorkshire, on the 12th day of December, 1866. And the day following, at Tunstall, in Staffordshire, one fearful and fatal explosion killed over one hundred of its husbands, brothers, and sons, calling forth the shrieks and heart-rending agony of its mothers, widows, and orphans. At the Lund Hill mines, in February, 1857, one hundred and eighty-nine were killed; and at the Hartley colliery, in January, 1862, two hundred and nine perished. All these are, indeed, fearful in the immense sacrifice of life, but Barnsley exceeds all colliery explosions on record, in this or any other land. The principal newspapers contained short telegraphic accounts of this deplorable accident, on the morning of the 13th, and the Queen telegraphed from Windsor anxiously requesting information, for she could always weep with those that weep. And when, on the 14th, full particulars were given, the whole country felt the shock. I had been on a distant journey, and while returning, read the account with painful interest, but saw the first mournful evidence of what had happened at the Guide Bridge Junction. There four middle-aged persons, evidently colliers, were waiting at the station for the train that would take them near the fatal mine. Deep sorrow on each countenance, and eyes red with weeping, plainly told a sad tale. Wishing to converse with them, I, in as kindly a tone as possible, said,—

"I suppose you are going to Barnsley, my dear friends?"

"Yes, Sir; we are all on a sorrowful errand," was the reply.

"Have you some relatives amongst those that are lost *V* I asked.

"We have each a son killed 1"

This painful answer, accompanied by a flood of tears, made me almost regret having spoken to them on the subject, and I felt I could not ask them any more questions.

There is a melancholy interest in visiting scenes memorable from some sad events. No spot in all the parks and squares of London arrests the mind, or calls forth so many associations, as the few square yards in Smitbfield, where the martyrs for the truth bravely met their fate. Oxford boasts many places sacred to the good and brave, but none to compare with the place where Bidley and Latimer triumphed in death. The chronicles of our sea-girt shores contain many accounts of fatal rocks and shoals, but none more to be remembered than the spot that wrecked the "Royal Charter;" and now the inhabitants of Yorkshire, and visitors, will ever regard with mournful interest this deep, dark sepulchre containing three hundred unburied dead.

And is not this right *i* Is it not well for the living that we are not indifferent to the memory of the dead 1 Sad thoughts are often the best thoughts; and to mourn on the spot where others have been made to mourn, draws nearer our sympathies and binds humanity in closer bonds. The house of mourning is sometimes better than the house of feasting.

Such were my thoughts, and such my experience, on the day I wended my way through Barnsley to the Ardsley Oaks Colliery, the scene of the terrible explosion. On nearing the place, I found the approach to the pit's mouth guarded by boards, rails, iron ropes, and policemen. On the boards were large placards, with the word, "dangerous. Seeking a shelter from the cold, bleak wind behind a low stone office near the pit, I watched, with feelings not to be described, the dense volumes of dun and dark smoke rolling from the hot, fiery depths, as from a great burning furnace. But, O! the thought—the sickening, appalling thought —that down that flaming gulf were the bodies of three hundred human beings, the husbands, fathers, brothers, and sons of heart-broken wives, mothers, sisters, and children, who were wringing their hands in the wildness of grief, agony, and despair.

While silently standing and sorrowfully looking on the scene, I was joined by several miners who had relatives and friends in the pit. Some of them had been present on the day of the explosion, and could tell of the fearful events. They said that, it being "making-up" day, more men were in the mine than usual; and a terrible making-up day it was.

It was about half-past one on the 12th, when terrific booming, followed by a tremendous rush of roaring air, black smoke, and broken timber, belched forth from the shaft. The convulsion shook the whole country, as if rent by a mighty earthquake. Immediately the inhabitants, in frantic terror, came running from all parts,—mostly women and children,—screaming as if bereft of reason, wildly asking for husbands and fathers. And well they might, for there were one hundred and thirty husbands and fathers down the roaring pit. These were followed by long lines of people running in from more distant parts, and soon the mouth of the pit was surrounded by crowds breathless with excitement, After the stunning effects of the awful explosion had a little subsided, a cry rose, "Can nothing be done *1*—can nothing be done *1*—let us go down and save the poor men if possible!" Volunteers for the perilous undertaking instantly presented themselves, even more than required; and down the sulphureous deep went a number of as brave men as ever existed. Eighteen were found alive near the bottom, but so blackened, burned, and mangled, that, on reaching the top, nearly all expired in great agony.

James Earker, one of those noble and brave volunteers, who had formerly worked in the mine, in a letter to me, gives the following sad story of his terrible eleven hours work, in bringing out the dead. His words are:—

"When we got to the bottom, the scene there was indescribable,—death and horror on every side. O how dreadful! But the thought of having a father and three brothers in the dismal mine, besides many comrades, drove all fear from my mind; so, without asking if there was any danger, I asked where my father and brothers were working. The place being named, off I went. O! how dreadful was the smell of sulphur, and the sight was heart-rending. Dead bodies of men, boys, and horses, lay on every side; but, with my soul lifted up to heaven in yearning prayer for help, on I went to seek for the living, yet almost without hope of finding any. I met with one of the volunteers, a bottom-steward, who had a son in the mine; we went together through smoke and damp, over fallen roof and broken timber, with beating heart and listening ear for the voice of a comrade, or anything to show the sign of life. But all was still as death. Still we went on and on, the smoke getting thicker and thicker, and nothing but death and destruction all around, but we were forced to return.

"When we got away, we saw the fire burning in the distance, near the road we had to pass, and put it out to save our own lives. This done, we got to the bottom of the pit, almost dead ourselves, with the sulphur and fiery damp. They brought us brandy and rum to revive us, but I had nothing but water; being a total abstainer, and behoving, at that time especially, that water was better and safer than spirits, I took nothing else all the eleven hours I was in those dismal mines, and I was in all the worst places. I found a small tin bottle, filled it with water, fastened it to my belt, and being ordered along with another man, to go with and take charge of other four explorers, we again went back to seek for my father and brothers. We got three hundred yards further this time, but again we met with the black damp. We had only about three hundred yards further to go, but we were forced to stop. I cannot express my feelings at this time, but I still prayed to God for help. After resting awhile, we tried again but could not go. Two went back to fetch some sheeting to take the fresh air with us, and we waited until they returned, While waiting, we shouted and listened, but no response,—all was painfully still. We had not been waiting long before the air began to waver: then all was as if life was put into everything, for all was on a move. Then came a rush of air that staggered us all, and brought the black damp over us. I got my cap in my mouth to keep it out, but it had nearly ohoked me. I fell down, and after a time feeling a little better, I got to my feet and ran for my life. I did not run far before I got into the fresh air; here I stopped, and called for my com-

panions to come on. I again prayed to God to have mercy and help me, and I felt He answered my prayer, or I should now have been numbered with the dead. It was a fearful struggle,—so dreadful that I cannot describe it.

"We again got to the bottom of the shaft; my comrades then left me and went up to the top. Brandy and rum were again offered me, but still I would not take any, but kept to water. Feeling I could not leave my father and brothers in the mine, I got another man to go with me to seek for them. Strengthened by the hand of my God, we got three hundred yards further up than before; but here we had to stop,— sulphur, smoke, and black damp, hot as a furnace. We lay down, Darkening, but still no sound. O! where was my father I— where my brothers? and how was my poor mother I Lord, help my mother! These were my cries, nor could I help it.

"On returning back we met the master and the engineers; they wanted to know what we had seen. We all tried to explore further, but were driven back to the bottom of the pit. Some wished me to go and see how my mother was; but I durst not see her, so I did not go up. I again filled my bottle with water, again prayed for help, and again set out. This time I got one thousand yards. 0! the sights I had to pass; some poor creatures had not a rag left on their bodies;. there were fifteen in one lot, all dead. Some of our company began to carry them out; but my anxiety to find my father and brothers overcame everything. I had been down nine hours, and could not have endured what I did but for Divine help. On going further I saw another and another of the slain. Then came thirty-seven all in one lot! This was a sickening and a dreadful sight: the lamp that I held seemed as if it were mourning;—it was just like a little speck. My three brothers were amongst this lot, all dead, cold, and stiff. O that one of them could have spoken to me!

"Thomas lay on his back; about two yards further was Andrew, laid on his face; William was next, poor lad, also lying on his face,—these two lay together. I cried out,—'O! what must I

do,—what must I do t O my mother! my dear, dear mother! what will she do when she gets to know the worst!' I fell on my knees and prayed to God that He would support my mother, strengthen her faith, and sustain her.

"I believed He had taken my father and brothers all to Himself, or I think I should have died on the spot. When sufficient help came, one after another were borne away to near the bottom of the shaft. My strength was now done. I was taken up the pit, about half-past two in the morning. Agreeing with some others to go down again at nine, I set off home. And now came the grief,— how could I tell my mother the truth? You may think how it would be, poor, dear mother! After telling her, my spirit seemed to die away, and I lay down completely exhausted. But rest I'could not, so long as my father and brothers were under ground. I returned again to the pit, went down, brought up my brothers, got them home, and had them laid out. My dear mother was stupefied and helpless. I requested her to let me go and again try to recover my father; she made no answer. I was putting on my cap to go down again, when the second terrible explosion went off. O! how I thanked God for this deliverance,—it was all His goodness. A few moments more and I should have been killed.

"Yours very truly,

"JAMES BARKER,"

It is scarcely possible to conceive anything more truly dreadful, than this simple narrative.

"When the second appalling explosion, reverberating like thunder, burst forth, followed again by the belching of dense volumes of smoke, and shivered timber from the two shafts, it produced the most bewildering effect. Another rush was made to the sad scene of this double disaster, and the most intense excitement prevailed. Again sorrowing relatives ran wildly about, their grief breaking out anew; for now all hope of one being saved was dashed to the ground; the men about the pits sat down in horror and stupefaction, or wept like children, for twenty-six more lives were now sacrificed. (There were twenty-seven in the pit, but one miraculously escaped.) And these twenty-six were the brave, courageous, generous volunteers that had gone down to seek and save their fellow-men! This second direful catastrophe was felt to be a calamity indeed; and the gloomy intelligence hung like a black cloud over the whole country.

There is something truly dreadful when, in the midst of the ocean's rolling, rising billows, and raging, roaring storm, to see the blue-light shot up into the riven clouds telling of a ship in distress; or the cry of the mariner, amidst the howling blast, when his vessel is tossed among the breakers. But when a band of fearless hearts man the life-boat, and push out into the wild, foaming deep, with the express object of saving the perishing, and are themselves engulphed in a watery grave, a still more intense and painful feeling is excited. Such were the men, and such the object, and such was the fate of those six-and-twenty heroes, the last who perished in this fearful calamity.

But had they perished —had these men of science and experience, these engineers, masters, men of position perished *I*—was there no hope? Some thought there was, and the cage was slowly lowered to the bottom, and, after a short pause, amidst inexpressible excitement, slowly drawn again to the top. *But it was empty I* the fiery foe had slain them all.

"The strif e is o'er; death's seal is set, On ashy lips and marble brow."

Explosion after explosion followed, which too plainly told that the mines were burning. Practical engineers advised the filling up of the pits to extinguish the flames; tens of thousands of tons of earth were poured down the shafts, and now Ardsley Oaks is one of the world's great sepulchres.

On leaving this never-to-be-forgotten spot, I met three young women, whose sad countenances plainly told they were amongst the sufferers. All their husbands were amongst the dead, and still in the mines; they were the widows of three brothers, and they requested I would call to see their mother-in-law,

Mrs. Winter, in Baker Street, who had five sons all dead in the burning pit. I felt great reluctance to intrude on the aged creature's hopeless sorrow, and yet I had a wish to comply with the request. I went to the wrong door, the house of a person named Evans, who, with swollen eyes and quivering lip, told me her husband and son were amongst the killed. On entering the house of Mrs. Winter, I found the aged mourner sitting in her arm-chair, near the fire; for several weeks she had been very poorly. At her desire, I sat down beside her, but felt that no words of mine could meet her case. Taking hold of her feeble hand, I said,—

"I have called to see you, Mrs. Winter, at the request of your daughters-in-law."

"Did you know any of my sons *V* she asked.

"No; I am a stranger," I replied,.," and am just returned from the pit."

"Do you think there is any hope that any of them will be saved?"

"I fear not, but I hope you will again see them all in heaven."

"Thank you; thank you; for that hope is all that is now left to me. Oh! my J ohn, Thomas, Duncan, Joseph, William, shall I meet you there? Ah! my dear William, he was my youngest,— only eighteen*;* and that morning, knowing that I was poorly, he brought my breakfast to my bedside, and said,—' Mother, is there anything I can do for you, before I go *V* Ah! he thought well of his mother, and he would have done anything for me. I had very little trouble with any of my lads. Whatever must I do now *I"*

"Well, my aged sister, there is only one hand that can bind up the broken heart. He knows your heavy sorrows, and He only can sustain you now, and I believe He will."

Before leaving the bereaved creature, I hired a neighbour to keep her company, night and day, for a month, as she feared being alone, for now she was the only person left in the house.

My next call was on the mother of James Barker the dear mother for whom he prayed when he found his three

brothers amongst the dead. She resided at No. 3, Ash Eow, Hoyle Mill. In this row of stone huildings, there are thirty dwellings, and, sad to relate twenty-eight out of the thirty had one or more of the family amongst the dead The angel of death had indeed visited these homes, and a great cry, like the cry of Egypt, had gone up to heaven. Groups of children many of them too young to understand their loss, were playing about the doors. One of these often asked "Mother, when will father come home? Others, a little older, looked on in silence. These dear creatures

Would no more run to lisp. their sire's return,

Or climb his knee the envied kiss to share.

I found Mrs. Barker with both hands pressed against her throbbing heart, seated on the sofa. James told her who I was, and she held out her hand, saying,.

"O, how glad my dear husband would have been to see you! Many times, when reading your book, has he wished to see you. I thank you for calling, f I know it would have pleased him very much.

"Your loss is very sad and very great, Mrs. Barker, but you do not mourn as those that are without hope*;* for your husband has long been a Christian, and you have taught your children the way to heaven.

"Yes, my husband has been a member of a Christian church thirty years. He loved his dear Saviour, and we have been trying to live for heaven. We have had piety at home, and I believe that, through faith in a crucified Saviour, all four are now in heaven. But O! the mysterious ways of Providence!"

"Yes; God does indeed move in a mysterious wayy and is His own interpreter; but He so far explains these mysteries, as to tell us that all things work together for good to them that love Him, and that what we know not now of these mysteries, we shall know hereafter."

And here I would observe, that during the day I had been so overwhelmed with the magnitude of the calamity, so bewildered with the scenes of desolation I had witnessed, that I was almost stupefied; I had never shed a tear. But the moment I left James and his mother, I burst out weeping, and was glad I could weep. But my tears were tears of sympathy and joy. Yes, of *joy,* to know that Mrs. Barker felt, amidst her terrible bereavement, that her dear husband and sons were now in paradise; and I could not help exclaiming to myself,—0, that all the mothers and widows who have lost their husbands and sons could say the same

My next visit was to the house of a man whose loss everybody seemed to mourn—Edward Cartwright. He was one of those brought up out of the pit dead, and had left a wife and three children. Edward had been for several years a lay preacher, and had laboured hard to do good amongst men of his own condition in life, and at least one of those killed attributed his conversion to Edward's instrumentality. His widow was sorely distressed. She told me of his great anxiety to be useful and to do good; how he often, in family prayer, besought the Lord to have mercy on all the miners, and prepare them for all the dangers to which they were exposed, so that if it was sudden death it might be sudden glory. She spoke after long pauses, and after one of these she said,—

"You sit in his chair, sir."

This thought was too much for her,— she became almost convulsed with anguish. But at parting she said, "My dear Edward is now in heaven, and I shall soon follow."

It is now pleasing to think that the week before he met his instant death, he was speaking to the people in "Thirty-row," about being prepared to meet their God, saying, "The last month of the year is now come, and we may not all see the first month of the next." Speaking at a church meeting a day or two previous to the explosion, he, after giving out the hymn,

"Earth has many a scene of sorrow," held up both hands, saying, "There will be an amazing difference when I have to exchange my dirty coal-pit cap for a crown in glory!"

Edward, that amazing change has

come to thee! Would that all that perished with thee had so bright a prospect,—and would that the voice of this sad calamity might induce many, but especially the miners, to be wise, and think of their latter end.

THOSE who are best acquainted with the young in our Sunday-schools and churches, have often witnessed the deep concern of youthful converts for their unsaved friends and relatives, especially their parents. Pardoned themselves, they have tho most intense desire that those they love should enjoy the same blessing; and, when they see them indifferent to religion, and neglecting their soul's salvation, their fear that they will perish often amounts to bitter agony. One of these, who was daily praying in private for the conversion of her father and mother, told her teacher that if it was a question whether she or they must be saved, she felt she would rather be lost herself, if her loss would secure their eternal safety. Only those who feel the value of souls, and who weep and pray for those they love, can ever understand this disinterestedness. David felt it for his wicked son Absalom; Paul felt it for the unbelieving Jews; and-Christ felt it for us all; and those who are the most like Him will feel the most concern for others. „He wept over the sin-smitten cities, and His true followers still mourn over those who reject heaven's mercy, and bring down destruction upon their own heads; and the young person mentioned in this narrative was for & time one of these mourners.

When Lucy became old enough to understand her condition in life, she found herself the child of parents greatly different in many respects,—especially in things of the greatest importance. Her father was a strong, healthy, labouring man, with wages barely sufficient for the requirements of their small cottage. He was not unkind, nor was he a drunkard, though, like too many, he had formed the bad habit of spending a few hours in the public house on the Saturday evening, and sometimes on club-night came home rather unsteady. He never attended a place of worship,—

not because he "hated parsons," nor because he doubted the truth of the Bible, or objected to religion, but because he cared, or seemed to care, nothing about divine things;—he was a neglector. When the Sundays were fine, he would go out to get what he called fresh air, rambling about the streets or fields. At other times he would sit in the house, reading history or the newspapers, or spending most of his time in lounging on an old oak couch, resting himself, as he often said, "until his back ached."

The mother of Lucy was rather tall, very good looking, orderly, clean, and industrious. She had been in the Sunday-school from a child, but it was not until after her marriage that she began to be concerned about eternal things, or to think seriously about being saved. She had then two young children, four and six years old respectively. Lucy was the eldest, and almost every Sabbath the mother and children might be seen sitting on a form near the church door,— a very humble place, but one the mother always preferred; for she went to the temple as the publican went, —his prayer was her prayer,—and she said that any place in the house of God was precious.

She did not remain long a weeping penitent,—earnest seekers seldom do; and when the sweet, melting power of saving grace diffused its purifying influence through her happy soul, it came like the still small voice. But her joy was deep, and one evening, in the fulness of her gratitude, she could not refrain from telling her husband and young children. The husband listened patiently, but made no reply; the children wept, but did not then understand why; but Lucy never forgot that night.

When Lucy was about twelve years of age she went to work at the mill, and it was about this time her mother's health began to fail. One evening Lucy and her little sister were talking in bed about how they loved their mother, and how good she was: the little sister said,—

"Lucy, I do think my mother looks more beautiful every day.''

"Yes, when she is not so pale; when

her cheeks are red, as they often are, she looks very beautiful," replied Lucy.

"But what does father say she must have the doctor for, Lucy 1"

"I cannot tell, except it be because she coughs so much," was the answer.

Little did these children know the import of their conversation; others, who knew something of the family history, saw another marked to fall. For several months the mother was able to attend to her housework, and she was frequently so much better that her friends rejoiced in hopes she might be spared. But this was not to be: little by little she lost strength, but, like thousands similarly afflicted, she thought when spring returned, she should be well again. She did not cling to life because she feared death. She loved her husband and children, and for their sakes alone she wished to live.

About this time an event took place, which we wish was more frequent. Several of the teachers of the Sunday-school where Lucy attended, had met together for the special object of praying that the Lord would send the convincing and converting influence of the Holy Spirit among the senior scholars. God heard their prayers, and many began earnestly to seek the Lord, and believed to the saving of their souls. Lucy was one of this happy number, and when her mother heard of this, her joy was great; and especially when her other child, Eachel, near eleven years old, began to ask what she must do to be saved. The mother was in raptures; and, had her husband been brought to seek for mercy, her cup of bliss would have been almost full.

It was at this period I became acquainted with this interesting family, learned what is already narrated, and witnessed most of what follows.

I had been addressing a large gathering of young people, after which many of them wished to speak to me on various subjects; amongst them was Lucy. She had a request from her mother that I would call and see her, if possible, before I returned to Eochdale. I called, and found her seated in a large arm-chair, carefully wrapped in a dark woollen

shawl. Near her stood a small table on which was her Bible, two half oranges, and a small basin of sago gruel. The cottage was very neat and clean; Lucy had done it all, for though she was not yet fourteen, her mother had trained her well. She had been forced to leave the mill to nurse her sick parent, and willingly she did her work.

When are we happiest? In the crowded hall,
When fortune smiles, and flatterers bend the knee?
How soon, how very soon such empty pleasures pall,
How fast such fleeting rainbow pleasures flee!
We are not happy there.

When are we happiest then? O, when resigned
To whatsoe'er our cup of life may bring;
When we can know ourselves but weak and blind
Creatures of earth, and trust alone in Him
Who giveth in His mercy joy or pain!
O, we are happiest then.

And such was now the happiness of Lucy's mother. The last enemy's dart had once again found its mark, and soon the victim would quiver and fall. But there was no murmuring, no repining, no doubts, no fears. She was dying, and she knew it; yet how calm, how composed, how unspeakably happy; and in the only way in which it is possible for any being to be truly happy. She was resting her soul, body, circumstances, and prospects on Jesus; and, as the golden orb of day, *on* a calm summer evening, when sinking down the western sky, gilds as he goes all around with glory, suggesting thoughts of grander glories still, so did this dying saint behold by faith her home prepared by Christ in the mansions of the blest, and, as she passed away, showed the same glorious path to heaven.

Lucy brought a low buffet and sat beside her mother's knee, eagerly catching every word we spoke. My words were few, for I felt I was in the presence of an experience I had yet to acquire. She told me of her own conversion, and of the

peace she had since enjoyed. She told me of the goodness of God in permitting her to see her two children, like Mary, choosing the "good part" in their early days. She then paused, and for a time was silent. I did not like to speak, for I saw she was under some deep emotion. Recovering herself a little, she said,—

"O, how I did want to see my husband saved before I died! I have long prayed for this, and I believe it will yet come." Then taking hold of Lucy's hand, she said, "Lucy, my child, I want you to promise me you will never give him up; never, no, never!"

Lucy buried her face in her mother's lap, weeping and sobbing, and, with an earnestness that showed it came from an overflowing heart, said,—

"Mother, I never will, I never will. O, mother, we shall all meet you in heaven!"

The mother, smiling through her tears, said,—

"Thank you, my child, for that promise. Your

A young sister will help you; and I leave you this as a legacy, especially to you, Lucy."

Let us not think lightly of this affectionate, dying mother's request to Lucy, or doubt the influence of early piety. Most of the brightest ornaments of the Church of Christ found the Saviour while young, and some of them while very young, and began to exert an influence for good amongst their youthful acquaintances, and especially amongst those of their own family. Had the church more confidence in early conversions, more faith in the power of saving grace to reach our children, many cheering harvests would spring up amongst those who once sung hosannas in the streets of Jerusalem to the world's Kedeemer. God did, and God can, from the mouths of babes and sucklings, bring forth praise.

We know a girl who, one Sunday morning, was getting ready for the school, when three wicked men called for her father to go with them to a dog-race on the moors. The father promised to follow them in a few moments. He sat down to his breakfast; but his child was so shocked at the thought of her father going to a dog-race, especially on the Sabbath-day, that she could not help weeping.

"What is the matter with you, Sarah 1" asked her father. The child went and leaned on his shoulder, and, putting her small, thin fingers through his rough hair, said,—

"Father, should you go to dog-races on the Sunday, will not God see you 1"

"Bless thee, child, how thee talks! Away with thee to the school, and never mind me," replied the father.

"I will, if you promise me that you will not go," she said, still stroking down his hair with her delicate fingers.

"But I told the men I would go," he replied.

"Yes, but God will forgive you if you do not go, but He will not if you do; and I shall cry all the day about you."

"Bless the child, how she talks! Away with thee to school, and I will not go."

She pressed both his cheeks with her small hands, and ran off to the school, happy as a little queen.

But that was not all; that same evening this little lady had hold of the horny hand of her father, leading him to the chapel. She could read better than he could, and found the hymn, and stood on the form to be high enough to see the words. Nor was that all: several months after, this man, when giving his experience, previous to being admitted a member of the church, mentioned his child's conduct that Sunday morning he was going to the dog-race, as the beginning of his concern for pardon. He expressed his thankfulness to the Almighty that he had such a child, and said he felt, that if he had gone to that dog-race, God would have taken the child from him.

Two months after I had called to see Lucy's mother, about twelve o'clock one evening, there was a scene in that humble cottage. The father stood at the head of the bed, holding the hand of his dying wife; Lucy and Rachel knelt at her side, in speechless sorrow, and two neighbours sat at a distance, silently looking on. There were a few last words faintly spoken: these last words were,—

"Dear husband, see in my greatest need what religion can do. I wished to see you a child of God before I departed, but I have left a legacy to my children, and, when I am gone, Lucy will tell you what it is."

Feebly, very feebly, were these words spoken, and her soul, in the company of the waiting angel, went away to glory.

For several months after the mother's death, Lucy's father was very regular in returning home. He went less to the public house, and once or twice attended the church with his two children. He had some suspicion what the legacy was that his dying wife had left, but did not ask. Lucy durst not yet tell him, and nearly two years rolled over before it was explained. Lucy did most of the home work; a little help from a neighbour on the washing day was all she required, and things were moderately comfortable. But there was this one thing, this one cause of concern,—father was not a Christian. Lucy sometimes thought he would never be saved; that he would grow harder and harder in his indifference, and this gave her great anxiety. But she held fast to the promise made to her mother; she did not and would not give him up.

About this period a circumstance occurred, that greatly encouraged her to persevere in praying for her father. She had a young, pious companion in the church, named Ellen, who had a careless, prayerless mother. Believing in the power of prayer, she had set apart ten minutes every day to plead with God for her mother's salvation. About seven o'clock every evening, the time she was most at liberty from her work, she went up-stairs to her bedroom, to ask again and again for the burning desire of her soul,—her mother's conversion.

The mother had witnessed a great change in her daughter. She was always affectionate and kind, but had been unusually so for many months. She never seemed weary in helping her mother in the house, and did everything very cheerfully. Often had she requested her mother to go with her to her place of worship, but there was always some ex-

cuse,—she never would go. Ellen's going up stairs about the same time each evening, surprised her mother. She had noticed that sometimes, when she came down, her eyes were red with weeping, and determined to know what was going on. One evening when Ellen was gone up, the mother took off her shoes, gently went about half way up the steps, and sat down to listen; she then heard in a soft, subdued, but earnest voice, words that sent a thrill through her whole soul.

On the following Friday evening, Ellen was quietly sewing by the fireside, and her mother was ironing. Without turning round, her mother said,—

"Ellen, have you been praying for me?"

Ellen was greatly astonished at this unexpected question. Her face grew red, and her eyes filled with tears, and, when able to speak, she said,—

"O, mother, I could not help it, I could not help it! I feel so concerned for your soul."

Soon after this, Ellen had the unspeakable delight to walk beside her mother to the chapel, and to see her become a member of the church.

When Lucy heard of this, she was more and more determined not to give her father up. She, too, had a set time for prayer, and often had so much faith that she was now expecting it every day. Had the father known of this, surely it would have softened his hard heart. And he did know at last, for one evening on returning home much earlier than expected, and finding the door a little open, he entered without being heard. He stood for a moment, wondering where his daughter was, and, hearing a voice up-stairs, he was on the point of calling out, but, on listening, he became fixed to the spot. Lucy, thinking no one but God heard her, was pleading for her father.

"O Lord," she said, "Thou knowest I promised my mother I would never give my dear father up; nor I never will. Thou saved my mother, Thou hast saved me and my sister, and Thou can save him. O Lord, do save my dear, dear father, and I will praise Thee for ever."

Fearing that Lucy might know he had heard her prayer, he silently stepped out, leaving the door as he found it, and set out on a short walk. But it was such a walk as he had never had before, and his thoughts were loud thoughts. "This is the Mother's Legacy," said he; "I thought what it was, but now I know. I have always thought my children the best children in the world, and now I think better of them than ever. But what shall I do 1 I cannot stand this; and yet, what shall I do 1"

So much of the family I knew, when circumstances separated us. Lucy's father lost his work, and had to remove into another county to get employment. Eleven years after, I was attending a religious gathering, and, in my address to the people, mentioned the Mother's Legacy. The moment I had done so, two females who sat near the platform, seemed greatly affected. I could not tell why, and feared I had said something wrong. After the meeting was over, these two females followed me into the vestry, and I at once recognized Lucy and Rachel, both dressed in black. I did not ask them any questions, for I feared their father was dead, and I well remembered the Legacy. Lucy suspected my thoughts, and smiling said,—

"I see you are afraid to ask about my father, Mr. Ashworth."

"I am, Lucy," I replied.

"Well, I know why . but you do not need, for we have good news. You saw us a few weeks before we removed into this neighbourhood. The last Sabbath we lived in the dear old place, my father went with us to the church, and wished us all to see mother's grave, before we went away. We all three stood round the spot in silence. My father, reading my mother's name, said, as if talking to her,—

'"You left a legacy to your children, Martha, aud I now know what it is, and thank you for it.'

"O how my heart did beat when he mentioned the legacy, and said he knew what it was! We had never told him,— how had he got to know 1 'That night, before retiring to rest, knowing it was the last day we should reside in the cot-

tage where we were born, and where mother had died, we were very sad. I had locked the door, and Rachel and I were just going up-stairs, when father said,—

"' Lucy, I heard your prayer for me on Tuesday evening, and then learned what mother's request was. I know you are both anxious I should go with you to chapel and be a Christian; don't give me up. Will you kneel down now and pray for me?'

"We did all kneel down, but we could not pray; we did nothing but weep, and we rose up, not having spoken one word. What a night was that for us all! The following Sunday we all three went to the new house of prayer, about one mile from this place, and during the sermon father was completely broken down. Soon after he found peace; and now we think he is one of the best and holiest of men, and we are a very happy family."

"When I saw you in mourning, I feared your father was dead," I observed.

"0 no, we are in black for our grandmother,—my father's mother. She was a good creature, and died in great peace. When she heard of my father's conversion, she was in ecstacies; and though she was seventyfive years of age, she said she was so glad that she felt as if she could leap over the house."

We have in this narrative another illustration of the passage—" sowing in tears, reaping in joy." And what a joy! To see those we love walking with us in the way to heaven, is amongst the highest pleasures we can know in this life. To feel that when we part here, we shall soon meet again, and be for ever re-united on the pearly plains of paradise, makes our prospects of heaven more heavenly still. All children may not see their parents saved, as in this case, but there are many thousands of cases where the child has been the instrument of the parent's salvation.

To those of my young friends who have parents out of the way, like Lucy's mother I would say,—never give them up Heaven has given us a promise as firm as the everlasting hills:—" All

things, *whatsoever* ye shall ask *believing,* ye *shall* receive." With a promise like this, is it not strange that more of our parents are not converted 1 Never give them up. When you are discouraged, and feel tempted to despair of their solvation, remember Lucy's Legacy. WHILE reading over the names in the old Bibleclass roll-book of our Sabbath-school, thoughts are often suggested both painful and pleasing. When James Kershaw, once a poor boy, but afterwards member of Parliament for Stockport, revisited the Sundayschool of his early days, and looked over the old classbooks to find his own name, he was much gratified to see that for seven years he had not been once absent when a scholar, and double that number of years when a teacher; and, while putting back the book into the desk, he expressed his conviction that his attachment to the Sunday-school, and his deep regard for the Sabbath, was the foundation of all his blessings, temporal and spiritual.

Give me a young man that has a deep regard for the Sabbath,—that reveres as sacred the Lord's day,—he may not, like Mr. Kershaw, become a member of the House of Commons, but, depend upon it, he will have no mean social position. From this will spring almost every other good; he shall "ride upon the high places of the earth." But show me a young man that thinks lightly of the Sabbath, and seeks worldly pleasures on that day,—he will soon think lightly of the school, the church, the Bible, and everything sacred, and blast his own prospects in life, sink down in wickedness, poverty, and often in crime. The young man whose name stands at the head of this sketch, is a painful, though far from solitary, illustration of this truth, as our Bible-class records can testify.

Edmund was about the same age as myself, and, along with others, sat with me on a good strong threeinch thick form, supported by six round legs. We had two teachers, attending each alternate Sunday. One of them was a tall, patient, red-cheeked man, with soft hands, kind words, and a loving heart. We called him Old James, and we all loved him. The other was a stern, bad-tempered man, with a stiok, which he took care to make us all well acquainted with. Some people say that you may flog a lad any time, for he is always either going into mischief or just coming out. Our stern teacher seemed to be one of this class of thinkers, for he laid on, right and left. Perhaps we deserved it; if so, we got it, but none of us liked it.

One Sunday morning Old James was talking to us about heaven. We had been reading the twenty-first chapter of Kevelation, and the old man seemed almost in paradise while he was reading and talking with us about it. Never before that day had I such a view of that happy place. Old James saw we were all affected, and he laid his soft hands on our heads, one by one, and besought us to be good lads, and keep holy the Sabbath-day, and then we should go to that glorious place of which we had been reading.

Most of us had taken our dinners to the school, for nearly all in that class resided two or three miles from the place. At noon we gathered round the large, warm stove, in the bottom of the Chapel, and began to untie our small linen handkerchiefs, to see what we had brought for dinner. I well remember mine was an apple-eake, the half of a circle, with the widest *selvedge* of any apple cake I had ever seen. But it is a queer cake a hungry lad will turn his back upon, so I began digging my teeth into the selvedge, wondering when I should get to the apples. But when I remembered that the cake was as good as my poor dear mother could afford to make, and that she had made the best of what she had to do with, that settled all my questions, and I finished it without a murmur.

As we sat round the stove, we began to talk about heaven, our morning lesson. Edmund said to me,—

"Johnny, does thou think thou will ever get to heaven *1*" "I hope I shall, Edmund," I replied.

"And where will thou sit in heaven;—with Old James, or with him with the stick *1*" Edmund asked.

"With Old James, to be sure," was my answer.

"So will I, and so will I," said the other lads, all round.

That day we were all very good, and made a bargain that we would always go to the school, and keep the Sabbath-day holy, as Old James had requested us.

Spring came, and with the spring came a great misfortune to Edmund;— he got a new swallow-tailed coat, or, as we called it, a jacket with laps. So long as he had only a round jacket, like the rest of us, he seemed all right, but the laps mado him quite a somebody. He thought and said he was too big now to go to the Sunday-school; so he left us and went away, taking his laps with him. It is a dangerous thing to turn some lads out of round jackets into laps, as Edmund's case proved.

It was many months before I met with Edmund again; but one Sunday evening, on returning from the school, I saw him in company with several others, who, twelve months before, he would not have been seen, with. He stood on the top of a hedge, a short distance from the highway, and, the moment he saw me, he put his hands to his mouth and shouted,—

"Amen! amen! let us pray;" and then, with his companions, burst out laughing.

I stood still and, looking at Edmund, said, speaking loud so-that he could hear,—

"Edmund, is this keeping the Sabbath-day holy, as you promised you would?"

But this only brought a fresh peal of laughter, with another, "Amen! amen!"

Young as I then was, I could see that Edmund made a great mistake when he thought he was too big to attend the Sunday-school. He had now become the companion of fools, and could mock at the Sabbath. It was easy to predict what would follow, for the way in which a person regards the Lord's day is always a test of character. It is God's day,— the Sabbath of the Lord. It was mercifully given to man,—to all men,—at creation; confirmed when the law was

given on Sinai; and the commandmont then written by the hand of God Himself, imperatively demanded it should be kept holy. It was made for man, that he, his son, his daughter, his man-servant, his maid-servant, the stranger, and even his toiling cattle should enjoy it as a day of rest. It was not given to the Jews only; it no more belongs exclusively to the Jews than do all the other commandments. The ten commandments are for all nations, and are binding to the end of time. "Till heaven and earth pass away, one jot or one tittle shall in no wise pass from the law, till all be fulfilled. Whosoever, therefore, shall break one of these least commandments, and shall teach men so, he shall be called the least in the kingdom of heaven." But it is doubtful if ever such a man, except he repent, get to heaven at all. Isaiah, when speaking of the blessed day, says, "If thou turn from doing thy pleasure on my holy day; and call the Sabbath a delight, the holy of the Lord, honourable: and shalt honour Him, not doing thine own ways, nor finding thine own pleasure, nor speaking thine own words; then thou shalt delight thyself in the Lord, and I will cause thee to ride upon the high places of the earth; for the mouth of the Lord hath spoken it." There is something more in these words than mere *resting;* but it was ordered to be a day of rest, that it might be better kept as a day of holiness. Yet this day, given by heaven as a blessing, is by thousands turned into a curse; for they are more wicked on this day than any other. And, though they have the advantage of ceasing from work on that day, because of the commandment, yet they hate its holy character. The infidels of France, during the reign of reason, terror, and bloodshed, abolished the Sabbath, but there was soon a terrible retribution. Let men say what they will, all the armies of Christendom cannot change one "Thus saith the Lord;" come to pass it must, and the events of every-day life amply prove it.

Todd, the American writer, tells us that every merchant in New York who kept his office open all or part of the Sabbath-day failed in business; that, in twenty years, at least forty Sabbath-breaking merchants went to ruin,—not one escaped.

In the neighbourhood of Rochdale, there is a place called Bridge Mill. A good old Christian, of the name of William Heape, rented this mill from a large and wealthy woollen manufacturer, of the name of Walmsley, residing at Castlemere. One Sunday morning, Walmsley sent Heape word that he must set all the men to work that day, and get ready some pieces that were much wanted. Heape returned for answer, that by one o'clock on the Monday morning he would begin, and do all he could, but he must be excused working on the Sunday. Walmsley was much offended at the answer, and sent his own warehousemen to do the pressing and packing of the pieces. The cart containing the goods had to pass through the brook called the Boach that ran close to the mill. The river had risen during the day, but, being night, they could not see this, and the horse, cart, and goods were all upset and carried down the stream. The warehousemen screamed out when they saw the cart turn over. Mrs. Heape, hearing them, ran out of the house to see what was wrong, and, seeing the goods floating down the stream, said,—

"There goes your Sunday work!"

The house and wealth of Walmsley have passed into other hands, but William Heape, the lover and observer of the Sabbath, greatly prospered, and his many sons, treading in their father's steps, have proved the words of Isaiah true.

Kings and rulers may take counsel together against heaven's laws, but He that sitteth in the heavens shall laugh at them. To go against a *Thus saith the Lord,* will bring inevitable ruin; and one *Thus saith the Lord* is, "Remember the Sabbath-day to keep it holy."

If it should be asked,—" But what has all this to do with Edmund?"—my answer is, that his subsequent life will show what misery a disregard of the Lord's day almost invariably entails. We saw him last standing on the top of the hedge, shouting and mocking one of his school-mates. Three other scenes in

his career will show the consequences of his early follies.

A rough, drunken character that sometimes attended the Chapel for the Destitute, came to request I would go to see a young man who was very ill in one of our lodging houses. He said,—

"I guess he is somebody's child, and should not be left to die like a dog. He says he knows you; come, go wi' me and pray wi' him, if he wants it; that will do no harm, at ony rate."

I at once went with the rough messenger, and found a young man doubled up with pain, in a miserable bed. He groaned, and entreated some one to put something warm to his feet. T immediately got the oven plate, wrapped in an old rag, and pressed it to his cold feet. This soon brought relief. I had not seen his face, for he covered his head with the bed-clothes the moment I went into the room, and seemed determined I should not know him. But the-rough man said to him,—

"Hold up thy face, Ned, and let Mr. Ashworth see who thee art. What art te feared on? He will happen buy thee a drop o' brandy; for thee needs something for inside as well as eawt."

The dirty sheet was pulled off Ned's face, and I found that Ned was my old Sunday school-fellow, Edmund. He had been drinking for several days, fell ill, and crept into a common lodging-house, as he thought to die; but care and nursing, all at my expense, brought him round. I bought him a shirt and a pair of stockings, and he began work again, thankful for the kindness shown him. He told me, during his sickness, that he never had attended a place of worship for years, but that he never saw people going to the chapel or church without envying them; that he was most miserable on the Sunday, and thousands of times had wished that he had followed the advice of Old James, and kept the Sabbath-day holy.

Poor Edmund! he envied those that he saw keeping the Sabbath holy, and going to the house of God; and well he might.

There are many beautiful scenes in this beautiful world, but there is one that

has to me the most cheering interest, and awakens the most joyous thoughts. I am not insensible to the silent but impressive language of God's visible universe,—the heavens, the everlasting hills, the majestic rocks, the woods, the dells, the fields, the flowers,—these fill the mind with deep emotions, and give birth to unutterable feelings. But there is a sight still grander, awakening emotions still higher and nobler, when, on the Sabbath-morn, we see the gathering of thousands of God's people, old and young, to their various Sions, to mingle their voioes in praises to Him whose voice called forth those glorious heavens, those hills, rocks, fields, and flowers. It is then that heaven seems nearest to earth, and the glories of the temple above are reflected in the temple below.

"How sweet a Sabbath thus to spend,
In hopes of one that ne'er shall end!"

The next time I saw Edmund, was under still more painful circumstances. I had been several days serving on the jury, at the Manchester Quarter Sessions, and, perhaps in consequence of my name beginning with A, was appointed foreman. There were many persons to be tried for stealing, and amongst tbe number I was sorry to find the name of my old Bible-class mate. The charge against him was that, along with three others, he had stolen a sack of malt. Edmund was the least guilty; he had nothing to do with the stealing, but part of the malt was found in a bag under his bed. The trial did not last long, for there was no doubt of their guilt. Being the foreman, it was my duty to pronounce the finding of the jury, and when the court cryer, with a loud voice, called out, "Gentlemen of the jury, do you find Edmund guilty or not guilty?" with a heavy heart I looked at Edmund. Our eyes met, and in his eyes I could read the workings of his soul; they plainly said, " Have pity on me!" A choking sensation rose to my throat, and I was very near breaking down before I could pronounce the word— Guilty!

The rest of the jury seemed surprised at my emotion, but I did not tell them that the guilty prisoner at the bar was once a happy, innocent lad in our happy

Sunday-school class. Edmund's sentence was six weeks' imprisonment, with hard labour.

Jurymen, after their work is done, have the privilege, if they wish it, of going through the cells, wards, and workshops of the prison. On this occasion we all agreed to go together, and see, what I am sorry can be seen, in any part of this country. I stood on a balcony, looking at a number of men, dressed in coarse, black woollen cloth, with yellow stripes, turning a large wheel with their feet;—this was the tread-mill. Edmund was one of these, and while I stood looking at the panting men, it was Edmund's turn to come off. He went straight to a pump that stood near, and taking hold of the chained tin cup, he drank deep and long, then wiped the sweat from his face, and sat down till his turn came again. It was heavy work, and I could not help thinking of the words, "The way of transgressors is hard." I felt truly sorry for Edmund, and was glad he did not see me, for I did not want to cause him pain by the wide contrast. I had not then, nor have I yet, anything of which I can boast; but I do believe that a love and constant regard for the Sabbath, has saved me from those snares into which many of my early acquaintances have fallen. After Edmund came out of prison, he was comparatively steady for many years. He kept away from thieves, but still most of his Sundays were spent in the public house. I had often invited him to attend some place of worship, and never again to touch one drop of drink. Again and again he promised to turn over a new leaf, but he did not. An old proverb says, that "the way to hell is paved with good intentions." Good resolutions, made in our own strength, are as weak as a straw.

Another message came,—this time brought by an old woman. She informed me that she had a man staying at her house, dying of consumption,—that he kept calling out,—" Will some one go and fetch John Ashworth? I am sure he will come if you tell him how ill I am. Do go and fetch him!"

We need not be surprised, when death stares the wicked man in the face, that he should be anxious for the company of praying men. When sickness lays a man on his bed, and, in the quiet hours, memory begins to travel back, and the black way-marks of life rise up to the vision,—when conscience can no longer be smothered, and the soul begins to realize and shudder at its gloomy prospects, one that knew something of this tells us that,—

"The Boui that broods o'er guilty woes,
Is like the scorpion girt by fire;
So writhes the mind remorse has riven;
Undone for earth, unfit for heaven;
Darkness above, despair beneath;
Within it fire, around it death."

I have long made allowance for the ungodly, even for the mocker and scorner at religion while in health, when the time of testing comes, as come it will, wanting the counsel and prayers of those they may have once slighted, but whom they now regard as the happiest of mortals, and would give a thousand worlds to be as they are.

These were my views and feelings when I entered the sick room of Edmund, for he it was that the old woman had fetched me to see. I was glad this time to find him in a clean, decent place.

"I am fain you are come, John, but you have only come to see a wreck,—a poor skeleton," were Edmund's first words.

"But why are you glad to see me % I fear I can do but little for you now, Edmund."

"But surely I must not die as I am,—unprepared, unprepared; surely not, surely not!"

"But I cannot save you, Edmund, nor all the men in the world; no, nor all the saints and angels in heaven."

"But surely I must be saved, John; what must I do? do tell me 1" "Do you believe you are a sinner, Edmund?"

"Yes, I do," was his reply.

"Do you feel that you are a sinner 1—for there is a vast difference between simply believing it and feeling it." "Yes, I do, John," he replied.

"Do you believe that Christ died for you, and that He can save you?"

"Yes, I believe He could, but I don't believe He ever will."

"Then there is no hope for you. If you don't believe He will save you, how can you be saved V "Well, then, I can never be saved; for I have been so wicked and sinned so long, and done it with my eyes wide open, for I knew better. Sabbath-breaking has brought me to this; that was my first wrong step. O that I could but undo what I have done; but this can never be! What must be done?"

"Believe that Christ will save you, Edmund," I answered.

"But how can I?—how can 1 I"

"Because He says He will, and you ought to believe Him, for if you don't you grieve Him."

"Where does Christ say that? Do tell me, John."

"You read many times in the Bible-class, at school, these words:—' Christ Jesus came into the world to save sinners,—He came to seek and to save that which was lost;' and to those that are burdened with sin, He says, 'Come to me, and I will give you rest.'"

I then paused, to let the merciful words of a merciful Saviour have their full weight. For a long time we were both silent; I feared to disturb his thoughts, for he was evidently surprised at what had been said. I took out my handkerchief to wipe the tears that were running down each side of his face, but still I spoke not. Heaving a deep sigh, he quietly turned his headi and, looking me in the face, slowly said,—

"Is it so 1—is there mercy for me?"

Seeing he was exhausted, I took my pocket Testament, read some portions suitable for his condition, and then knelt down to plead for poor Edmund. 0 how precious to me was the sinner's Eriend at that moment.

During that night Edmund was taken with a fit of coughing, and burst a blood vessel; and, when I called the following morning, I saw a worn-out body covered with a white sheet. Edmund was dead.

Do I think he was saved 1 the reader will anxiously ask. I dare not answer the question. The Judge of all the earth will do right, but if the Sabbath-breaker take warning, my object will be answered in writing this narrative of my old school-fellow, Edmund. /. *H. Micklem & Co., Printers, Manchester.*

9 781230 459875